The Study of Religion
in
American Universities

Ten Case Studies with Special
Reference to State Universities

By Robert Michaelsen
Professor of Religion and Director of the School
The University of Iowa

Published by

The Society for Religion in Higher Education
400 Prospect Street
New Haven, Connecticut 06511
1965

TABLE OF CONTENTS

iii

TABLE OF TABLES

PREFACE

This is an examination of provision for the study of religion in the curricula of ten American universities. Its primary purpose is to describe the curricular program in religion in each of these institutions, and to analyze each program, in terms of its rationale and the view of the subject matter entailed. The primary focus is on examining the formal policy and program which exist at present for the study of religion in the institutions considered. This includes insofar as information was available a survey of the history and design of each program, the courses offered, patterns of specialization, enrollments in selected courses, faculty appointments—both those made and those contemplated, and areas of specialization and competence represented within each faculty. An effort is made, briefly in the Introduction, to set the study of religion in the American university in historical context; to discuss possible legal implications of the study of religion in state universities; to discuss the nature of religion as an academic field; and to deal with questions having to do with the organization of a curricular program in religion. The Conclusion suggests steps that might be taken to advance the scholarly study of religion, given the present situation.

Certain principles of selection operated in the choice of the ten institutions included in this study. Eight of the ten are state universities. This type of institution is growing in importance on the American educational scene, as a growing percentage of students who continue their education beyond the secondary school is to be found in tax-supported colleges and universities and as more state universities become major academic institutions. The study of religion quite obviously confronts the state institution with peculiar problems. The most obvious of these has to do with possible implications of state and federal constitutional provisions with regard to religion. The close relationship of the state university to the people of the state, with all that this implies about varieties of types and degrees of religious affiliation and commitment, is also a factor of no small importance. Furthermore, many state universities, including land grant institutions, developed primarily in response to the practical needs of the people and thus have tended to be strongest in vocational, technological, and professional areas and not particularly strong in liberal arts. This has had a definite effect on the manner in which the study of religion

v

has been approached. While some form of curricular work in religion is offered in most public institutions of higher education in America, full and systematic study of religion has been conspicuously absent in nearly all of these schools. More recently, however, many state universities have been in the process of examining their responsibilities with regard to the question. A study which places heavy emphasis on the state university is warranted, then, because of their increasing importance in American higher education and because of the special circumstances relating to the study of religion in them. Such a study might also prove helpful in a practical way by showing in some detail what is actually being done in several schools.

There are, however, obviously many elements associated with the study of religion which are common to both state and private institutions. These include such questions as the nature and scope of religion as an academic field and the type of structure best suited to the development of a curricular program in religion. Thus while this study focuses primarily on state universities, it includes two distinguished private institutions—Princeton and Stanford—which have developed distinctive curricular programs in religion.

The majority of institutions described are universities of national and international reputation. This selection was made deliberately on the assumption that distinguished institutions tend to be looked to as pace-setters. However, the institution without a long history, established traditions, and wide reputation is sometimes in a better position to engage in bold experimentation than is the more established school—especially if such experimentation appears to involve some departure from patterns of the past or accepted ideas about what is appropriate. Thus two "emerging universities" — Western Michigan and the University of California at Santa Barbara—are included in this study because they have managed to develop curricular programs in religion which are of considerable substance and promise.

Selection was made with an eye to including a variety of approaches to the study of religion. These approaches range from one involving little formal attention to the development of a curricular program in religion (The University of California at Berkeley) to one involving a full-scale department with a staff of ten men with professorial rank offering courses and programs for the undergraduate non-specialist, the undergraduate major, and leading to the Ph.D. degree in religion

(Princeton). They include an interdepartmental program in religion under the guidance of a faculty committee (Michigan); a similar program in comparative religion utilizing existing courses in various departments plus courses taught by professors from an independent school of religion (Indiana); departments staffed by men of professorial rank (North Carolina and Western Michigan); a department staffed by selected campus clergymen and some university faculty (Michigan State); an institution which allows a limited amount of credit for elementary level Bible courses taught in denominational "Bible chairs" and by men without faculty status (Texas); a program in religious studies which is developing into a department (University of California at Santa Barbara); and a special curriculum in religious studies under the aegis of a humanities section in the School of Humanities and Science (Stanford). Some of these programs concentrate primarily on the Western religious heritage or the major religions of the West, while others provide more opportunity for study of the major non-Western religions than for the study of Judaism or Christianity. Some have endeavored in some way to take seriously America's religious pluralism—by devoting some attention to Jewish and Roman Catholic studies, for example—while others evidence no obvious attention to this factor. In some institutions without a department or a core of scholars in religion, the study of religion is carried on solely in and through such departments and disciplines as sociology, anthropology, history, philosophy, languages and literature. Other institutions have employed scholars with a primary competence in religion—historians of religion, philosophers of religion, theologians, and Biblical scholars.

Such variety is instructive, and not necessarily unfortunate. American universities are not universally standardized, nor should they be. It has not been my intention to elevate any single approach as the standard. Nevertheless, I have not avoided evaluation and critical analysis, and while one program is not necessarily standard, every program can and should be assessed in terms of its own internal consistency and its adequacy to the field.

Because regional variations may be of some importance in this area as in others, an effort was made to select universities from most of the major regions of the United States. At the same time, the selection of three state universities from one state (Michigan) and of two campuses of the University of California affords some opportunity for comparison of patterns within single states.

Ten institutions do not and cannot represent American higher education. While the study has some implications for types of educational institutions other than universities—such as state colleges, teachers' colleges, and liberal arts colleges—no effort was made to deal directly with these. I regret that it was not possible to include in the study a number of other universities with curricular programs in religion. It would be instructive to examine carefully more institutions with departments of religion of long standing, such as Oregon and Florida, and also recently created departments such as the one at Pennsylvania State. The University of Illinois has for more than forty years granted credit for courses taught in religious foundations, but this practice has recently been subjected to faculty analysis and questioning. The faculty of the College of Arts and Sciences has rejected a faculty committee recommendation that a department of religion be established within the College. Instead, the faculty accepted a recommendation that an interdepartmental committee be created to coordinate religion courses within the University. The status of the courses offered by the religious foundations continues to be an uncertain one.

Independent schools of religion have had a long history of offering course work for credit at such institutions as Kansas and Missouri. The School of Religion at the University of Iowa (Iowa City) has existed since 1927; has within its faculty various religious orientations, including Jewish, Roman Catholic, and Protestant; and is fully integrated within the University in terms of curricular structure. Iowa is also the one state university in the nation that grants the Ph.D. degree in religion.[1] The University of Wisconsin recently instituted a Ph.D. degree program in Buddhist studies. These and other institutions and developments are of interest to any examination of curricular programs in religion with reference to state universities. But necessary limitations dictated a study of modest proportions, and it seemed best to concentrate in some detail on a limited number of institutions.[2]

This study is based on work done during the 1963-64 academic year. Information was gathered through catalogues and other relevant printed materials; through correspondence; and through brief visits to the universities included in the study. The conclusions presented are my own, reached after review of these relevant materials and first-hand observation. The essay is more impressionistic than statistical in nature. (The only figures consistently listed for each university are those having to do with enrollments in selected courses.) Furthermore, little effort has been made to compare the various institutions in any statistical sense since such an attempt would encounter considerable difficulties due to the individual differences between the universities involved. Wherever possible, the information given extends through the Spring semester or term of 1964.

The study was carried on in connection with a special project of The Society for Religion in Higher Education. Since its incorporation as The National Council on Religion in Higher Education in 1923, the Society has given continuous attention to the area of religion in higher education. This particular project was initiated in response to the present rapid growth in public higher education, and was under the supervision of an Advisory Committee consisting of Dr. John W. Ashton, Vice President and Dean of the Graduate School, Indiana University; Dr. Luther Harshbarger, Professor of Humanities and Religious Studies, Pennsylvania State University; Dr. J. Alfred Martin, Jr., Danforth Professor of Religion in Higher Education, Union Theological Seminary; Dr. Lynn White, Jr., Professor of History, University of California at Los Angeles; Mr. Lawrence P. DeBoer, Executive Director, The Society for Religion in Higher Education, *ex officio;* and myself as Project Consultant for 1963-64.

I wish to express my appreciation to the Advisory Committee, to The Society for Religion in Higher Education, to the Graduate College of the University of Iowa for granting me the status of Research Professor for the Fall semester, 1963-64, and to the administration of this University for granting me a leave of absence during the Spring semester of 1964. Appreciation is also due to the Lilly Endowment for a grant which made the first year of the Society's project possible, and to the administrators and faculty members of the ten universities who gave me invaluable assistance in conducting the study and extended gracious hospitality to me during my visits to their institutions. To the latter I wish especially to indicate that insofar as I have expressed critical conclusions concerning the curricular programs in religion in their institutions I have not intended these critical analyses to refer to any particular individuals but rather have attempted to assess the curricular programs in religion in terms of my understanding of their inner consistency and their adequacy to the field of religion and to the responsibilities of a university in this field.

Responsibility for the conclusions of the study is my own, and these conclusions do not represent an official position of the Advisory Committee, The Society for Religion in Higher Education, or the universities involved.

ROBERT MICHAELSEN

Professor of Religion and
Director of the School of Religion
The University of Iowa

Iowa City

    December, 1964.

---

1. Iowa was not included in this study because of my own years of involvement in the Iowa program and my present status as director of the Iowa School of Religion.

2. For a brief description of the programs of twenty-five institutions see Milton D. McLean and Harry H. Kimber, *The Teaching of Religion in State Universities* (Office of Religious Affairs, The University of Michigan, Ann Arbor, 1960).

INTRODUCTION
THE STUDY OF RELIGION IN AMERICAN UNIVERSITIES:
With Special Reference to State Universities

Trends

The study of religion is not something new to American higher education. The tradition of Christian humanism lies deep in our history. And that tradition generally involved the required study of the classics of Greek, Latin, and Hebrew Literature, including the Bible. It also included systematic grounding in the theological or philosophical-theological system of the time. Such was the practice in the Colonial colleges. And required courses in such areas as moral philosophy, natural theology, and "Evidences of Christianity" were a common feature in nearly all American colleges, including state schools, until after the Civil War.

During the second half of the nineteenth century, however, the curriculum of Christian humanism went into decline. The older tradition with its emphasis on breadth, wholeness, and the development of the Christian "gentleman and scholar" gave way to the emphasis of the German universities on depth, specialization, and scientific objectivity. At the same time, theology, which had been considered important enough to be of interest to all students in the early American colleges, became a minor enterprise of little or no importance in the majority of developing American universities. On the one hand, defenders of orthodoxy became uneasy about college and university encroachment upon what they regarded as their preserve and sought to protect the truth and purity of theology by carrying it on in the relatively isolated atmosphere of the seminary. (Most American seminaries developed under denominational control and were not associated with a university.) On the other hand, while American universities were strongly influenced by the German university experience and pattern—a pattern which included faculties of theology—theology was not a commonly accepted discipline in the developing American university. In fact, most American universities developed in an intellectual atmosphere which was quite hostile to theology.[1]

Thus the study of religion took on a decidedly different character in American universities in the late nineteenth century. Religion now became the object of study by specialized disciplines. Scholars turned from a preoccupation with theological statements and a study of the sacred scriptures in a theological context to a study of such matters as origins, comparative relationships, and details of historical development. While theology declined as an academic discipline, such disciplines as comparative religion, semitics, psychology of religion, and sociology of religion either came into existence or underwent dramatic development in this period, and historical-critical methods were applied to the study of the Bible on a hitherto unprecedented scale. So great was the activity in these areas that one might well refer to the period between 1890 and 1910 as the "golden age" of American scholarship in religion.[2] Looking forward into the century from the context of 1910 one might have expected a continued flourishing of such scholarship. But such in fact did not occur, and by the mid-1930's the technical disciplines associated with the study of religion occupied a relatively unimportant place in most American universities while the earlier attention to religion as a part of general education had also declined seriously. Thus while universities experienced dramatic growth in the intervening period, and some academic disciplines flourished, this was not true of the study of religion.[3]

Religion studies faced special difficulties in the emerging state universities, where often a strong liberal arts or classical humanistic tradition had never existed and where constitutional limitations appeared to restrict what could be done in this area. Theology rarely received formal academic attention in these institutions, and such areas as church history, history of religions, and Biblical studies were commonly neglected or grossly underdeveloped. A few state universities—such as Michigan and California—did develop significant work in areas related to the study of religion, such as anthropology and Near Eastern studies, but most of the state schools contributed little to the advancement of scholarship in religion. At the same time, efforts were made to provide studies in religion in some state universities through some type of extra-university structure. Denominational groups founded "Bible chairs" or set up some other type of device whereby students could take courses which were accredited either directly by the university or through some kind of transfer procedure. Such courses were almost always taught by instructors who did not have faculty status in the university and were offered in an off-campus setting. Independent schools of religion were established at some universities in order that students could study this area which was not available to them in the university. Such extra-university structures were often represented as offering a legitimate solution to problems stemming from the American tradition of separation of church and state. They were also sometimes regarded as bridges between the religion of home and church and the atmosphere of critical inquiry which characterizes the university. Such approaches contributed—and still contribute—to the study of religion in some state universities, but this sort of pattern was not adopted by a significant number of state universities. Furthermore, such an approach tended to put religion in a special category by itself—outside or alongside regular university curricular offerings and taught by instructors without full status in the university. The very existence of such independent structures bore witness to the effect that the university as such could not or would not include religion within its regular curricular program and structure.

The trend more recently has been for religion studies to assume a more normal place in the curricular structure of the university, including some state universities. During the past twenty years departments of religion or special curricular programs in this area have been established in a significant number of American universities, including eight of the ten considered in this study. In fact, it appears that American universities have been giving more serious attention to the study of religion in the past two decades than they had since early in the century. And in the case of state universities the recent interest in this area is unparalleled in American history.

At the same time, there has been an upswing of scholarly attention to and research in religion in all sorts of institutions and by scholars in various disciplines. A growing number of historians, and especially intellectual historians, has become interested in the area. Students of culture, especially of both primitive and non-Western cultures, have turned their attention to religion with renewed interest. The increased interest in non-Western cultures has quite naturally produced an accompanying increase of interest in the major non-Western religions; and it is quite possible that we are today on the threshold of a major development in this type of study. Such sub-disciplines as the sociology of religion and the psychology of religion have developed more significantly in the past decade than in any previous period since early in the century. The theological "renaissance" of the 'thirties and 'forties has brought about an increasing interest in theology and in theological scholarship. The moral, philosophical, and historical probings of such dominant figures as Paul Tillich and the Niebuhr brothers

(Reinhold and H. Richard) have exercised a massive influence upon trends in theological scholarship and also have stimulated interest in the study of religious issues and phenomena in such widely scattered areas as philosophy, psychology, sociology, history, political science, and literature. Thus we are today in a period of major development in the study of religion in American universities and of a flowering of scholarship in this area not unlike that which occurred at the turn of the century. At the same time it appears that theology is being treated with renewed seriousness as an area of scholarly inquiry and as an academic discipline.[4]

Issues

These recent developments have brought a number of issues into focus, ranging from broad questions about the responsibility of the university for the study of religion to specific questions about organizational and structural detail. Some of the more pressing of these questions include: Is religion a legitimate field or area for the university, and especially for the state university, to include in its formal curricular structure? What is and should be the purpose of such study? What is its nature? Is there an academic discipline of religion? If not, what are the disciplines peculiarly fitted for the study of religion? Is theology a legitimate academic discipline? Who will teach in the curricular program in religion? Where should the primary focus of the study of religion be—on our own religious heritage or on the major world religions; on Biblical studies or on religion and culture; on historical or on contemporary issues? Should such study be organized on a departmental basis or in some other fashion?

There appears to be no single answer to any one of these questions. Indeed, if one seeks proof of the reality of pluralism in American higher education he can find it in the variety of ways in which the subject of religion is approached academically. This variety is not surprising when one considers the history of American higher education and the complexity and controversial nature of religion. Nor is it necessarily to be deplored. But this is not to suggest that there are no standards to be applied. In fact, experience and some knowledge of history and recent developments might lead one to conclude that appropriate academic standards are much needed in this area.

The question of the legitimacy of the study of religion in the university is of no small moment. It is raised both within religious communities and within universities. On the one hand, religious communities have tended to guard rather jealously their own prerogatives in the area of education in their faith, and generally speaking have not looked with favor upon the university which has sought to engage in the teaching of religion—especially if this tends to raise doubts about the truth and authority of their faith. On the other hand, some within the academic community have associated the study of religion with indoctrination, or with something other than a scholarly approach, and have considered it best for the university—especially the state university—not to become involved in a subject that is so controversial and so heavily freighted with emotion.

The question of the legitimacy of the study of religion in the university has been most often debated in the context of the state university. This "institution of people" has been caught in a peculiar "bind." It has been charged with being "godless" either because it does not "teach religion" or because it teaches irreligion. In some instances it has tended to avoid the area of religion for legal or public relations reasons and in others it has entered into quasi-academic arrangements under which religious groups themselves have taught courses in this area.

But in the final analysis the question of the legitimacy of the study of religion in the state university is not a public relations or even a legal matter but an educational and academic one. On such grounds, it has been argued that any university, including a state university, should afford ample opportunity for the study of religion because it is a major aspect of human life and culture and the university's task includes study of the nature, function, characteristics, and history of human cultures and intelligent concern for major issues of human life. Religion is a massive reality in human history and present-day society. No other reason appears to be needed to justify its systematic study in the university. Furthermore, it has been suggested that constitutional provisions or court opinions do not appear to preclude such study in state universities. In fact, recent U. S. Supreme Court decisions in the area of church and state and religious freedom seem to grant the legitimacy of the study of (or teaching *about*) religion in tax-supported institutions, and constitutional lawyers seem almost universally to agree that such study has a rightful place. The most important single point is that such study be academic or educational in nature rather than devotional or indoctrinational.[5]

It is not surprising that educators should raise questions about the legitimacy of the study of religion since such study has often been seen primarily as a form of edification or as a means of producing piety or making men better morally. Historically, the study of religion has been closely associated with the purposes of the religious community—such as edification, passing on the heritage, and even worship. Frequently the study of religion has been justified in American colleges and universities on other than academic grounds and its purpose has been seen as being other than intellectual in nature. Whether or not the study of religion might make the student more religious or more moral may be a question worth study in itself. But ambiguity can be avoided and false hopes dispelled with a careful insistence that the primary purpose of both the university and the study of religion is learning, understanding, discovery—is intellectual rather than moral or religious. And in recent years those charged with developing curricular programs in religion in both state and private universities have stressed the scholarly or academic approach with just such a purpose in mind. Thus the Princeton University faculty committee which urged in the mid-1930's that a clear distinction must be made between the study and the practice of religion was stating a principle which has tended to serve increasingly as a standard for all university study in this area.[6]

If the legitimacy of the study of religion in the university is evident and its primary purpose is seen as being intellectual, the next question has to do with methodology and procedure. This question is not an easy one to answer because of the complexity and pervasiveness of religion as a phenomenon and the apparent difficulty involved in defining religion as a field of academic inquiry. Religion is sufficiently pervasive as a human activity that its study is of concern to various academic fields and disciplines. And the study of religion may be a quite natural aspect of the work of sociologists, anthropologists, historians, philosophers, etc. But the problem that often faces the university in considering its total curricular program in religion is whether there is a *special* academic field of religion, and if so, whether this field is sufficiently well-developed to warrant a place alongside other fields in the university.

"Religion," like "art," is a term which is often used in a double sense; that is, to describe a human activity and to designate the specialized study of that activity. There does not appear to be any specific academic *discipline* which can be labeled "religion" as such, just as there is apparently no specific academic discipline which can be called "art." What, in fact, does exist is a variety of specialized approaches to phenomena called religious or artistic or to the phenomenon of religion or the phenomenon of art. And, in the case of religion, one can distinguish broadly between those scholars who are concerned directly and primarily with religion as a phenomenon and those who come to its study indirectly or secondarily. The former attempt to see religion synoptically or as an integral whole. They seek initially to understand religion on its own ground. And the methodologies they employ are determined in part by the nature of the phenomenon. The latter approach the phenomenon indirectly, that is, as a function of or a factor in something else, such as culture, or politics, or literature, or psychology. In their case, the methodology is determined by the larger or more fundamental context, such as culture, or society, or the human psyche, or by some other phenomenon or subject, such as literature, or politics, or art.

As an academic field, then, religion can be understood as involving those scholars who are concerned primarily with the direct study of the phenomenon of religion. As this field has developed in the academic world it has included such divisions as the following: history of religions, comparative religion, and phenomenology of religion; specialized studies in various religious traditions such as Buddhism, Islam, and Judaism; Biblical studies, involving the application of historical, archaeological, linguistic, literary, and theological methodologies to the study of the Bible; and theological studies, which have consisted of analyses of the historic and contemporary affirmations of the Christian church or churches and of critical, analytical, and synthetic approaches to religious faith as a human activity. Whether or not the university organizes its curricular program in such a way as to provide for the recognition and development of this broad academic field of religion, scholars are at work in these various divisions of the field and significant scholarship has been produced in all of them.[7]

The nature of the field and of the scholarship associated with it can be illustrated by a brief examination of two disciplines or areas —the history of religions and theology. Scholars at work in the history of religions are still engaged in an attempt to define their discipline, and the discipline itself is still in an early state of maturity—in America at least. But these scholars claim that the history of religions is a substantial discipline in its own right, a discipline which not only utilizes the historical method and the findings of such sub-disciplines as the sociology and psychology of religion, but also involves a methodology fitted specifically to the field of study; i.e., religious phenomena. Such phenomena do not stand by themselves. They always occur in a context. Professor Mircea Eliade, one of the leading historians of religions in America, points out that "there is no such thing as a 'pure' religious fact. Such a fact is always *also* a historical, sociological, cultural and psychological fact, to name the most important contexts." But, Professor Eliade suggests, neither the sociological, nor the literary, nor the psychological can do full justice to the religious phenomenon. What is needed additionally is a recognition of the phenomenon *as religious,* an attempt to come to grips with "the one unique and irreducible element in it—the element of the sacred." This "irreducible element" is, then, the point of focus for the historian of religions, and his methodology is designed to enable him not only to report the phenomenon but also to make some effort to understand it. This appears to require the same kind of combination of technical skill and empathetic approach as is required in the study of art or literature. The scholar must know the relevant language or languages and be familiar with the relevant context or contexts, and he also endeavors to use these skills and this knowledge in such a manner as to understand the phenomenon on its own ground or "from within." In discussing the methodology of the history of religions, Eliade draws an analogy with the history of art:

> A work of art reveals its meaning only insofar as it is regarded as an autonomous creation that is, insofar as we accept its mode of being—*that of an artistic creation*—and do not reduce it to one of its constituent elements . . . or to one of its subsequent uses. . . . In the same way . . . a religious datum reveals its deeper meaning when it is considered on its plane of reference, and not when it is reduced to one of its secondary aspects or its contexts.[8]

It is possible to distinguish between "horizontal" and "vertical" studies in the history of religions—that is, between those which focus upon elements of commonality ("universals"), or a particular type of phenomenon found in various religions, and those which concentrate upon one particular community of faith. Studies of the former type represent an effort to develop a "phenomenology of religion," to see "religion in essence and manifestation," to analyze and describe the various types of religious phenomena as they occur in a variety of contexts.[9] Studies of the latter type concentrate upon religious phenomena as they occur in one particular community or tradition.[10]

Theology is an intellectual enterprise in Western culture which is at least as old as Christianity and which was the result in early Christianity of a fusion of Greek and Hebrew thought patterns in the efforts of Christians to articulate and explain or defend their faith. Similar efforts also gave rise to the systematic development of theology in Islam and, to a lesser extent, in Judaism. This enterprise has experienced various fortunes in modern times, including a serious challenge to its validity stemming in large part from the development of modern science. In America, as suggested above, theology has been at most a peripheral enterprise in the life of the university. And it continues to be regarded with suspicion by many in the university— because of its historic association with a community of faith and its presumed unscientific nature. Thus the questions of whether theology is a legitimate academic discipline and of whether it should have a place in a curricular program in religion can be and sometimes are hotly debated. However these questions may be resolved in particular instances, it does appear that a significant amount of theological scholarship has been produced in recent times. And some would argue that both the theological enterprise and the university would profit from a closer association.

Rather than attempt an abstract definition of theology it is perhaps more helpful to describe briefly what theologians do as men engaged in intellectual and scholarly inquiry. The recent upsurge of activity in theology has been closely associated with such names as Barth, Bultmann, Berdyaev, Buber, Maritain, Niebuhr, and Tillich. While there is no unity of position or even of approach that holds these men together, the common thread that runs through the work of all of them is an effort to understand and explain religious faith and life. To this end these theologians make use of the tools and resources at hand—linguistic, critical-historical approaches to literature regarded as authoritative, creeds and confessions of a community of faith, confessional statements of men of faith, and the systematic statements of their predecessors and contemporaries. The work of some of these men is more narrowly technical while that of others is more synthetic or creative. Most of those listed have produced scholarly works of both types. Karl Barth, e.g., is widely known for his *Church Dogmatics*, a prime example of the latter type. But he has also produced one of the most scholarly works on Protestant theology in the nineteenth century, and even his multi-volumed *Church Dogmatics* is packed with analyses of Biblical and historical materials. Or consider Rudolph Bultmann, in effect both a New Testament scholar and a systematic theologian. While he gained his fame as a scholar through his development and application of form criticism (*Formgeschichte*) —

essentially a literary-critical device—he has more recently created considerable stir in theological circles with his emphasis on "demythologizing" the Christian message, an emphasis which, because it involves a radical re-examination of primitive Christian views in the light of twentieth century understandings of the nature of man and the physical universe, has far-ranging implications for constructive or systematic theology.

All of the men listed above were born late in the nineteenth century and have carried on their major work in the first half of the twentieth. All of them are or have been academicians. They have been widely influential in theological and other circles, and their work continues to be emulated by younger men. Thus the theological enterprise is a lively one in our time.[11]

A discussion of theology and theologians raises in its most acute form the question of who will teach in the curricular program in religion. Obviously the university must insist that scholars staff such a program. And presumably this could include scholars of the type described above—i.e., those engaged primarily in the direct study of religious phenomena as well as those who are interested in such phenomena secondarily or in connection with a primary interest in another type of phenomena. But will theologians or theological scholars be included in such a program, and will they be included *even* in a state university? Opinions differ radically on this question. On the one hand, there are those who claim that insofar as theologians are involved in some sort of personal relationship with a community of faith or have some kind of personal faith commitment which is of importance to their intellectual inquiry, they do not belong on the faculty of a university committed to objectivity in matters of intellectual inquiry and to neutrality in matters of faith. On the other hand, others claim that just such personal involvement and commitment are essential to the full and intellectually honest consideration of a particular religious faith. Those who hold such a position usually argue that a properly staffed curricular program in religion—whether in a private or a state university—should include theological scholars of various religious persuasions.[12] Some argue this latter position on what might be called sociological grounds—that is, that the curricular program in religion should be broadly representative of the varied religious complexion of the community at large and thus in America should include Jewish, Catholic and Protestant scholars. Others argue on what might appear to be somewhat more acceptable scholarly grounds—that is, that an adequate understanding of the meaning and of the various nuances of a religious faith requires an ability to identify with the perspective of that faith. Whatever the merits of these various arguments, it would appear that to insist that a scholar in religion either *must* or *must not* share the faith about which he teaches is to create problems for an academic community which has struggled toward the elimination of religious tests for faculty members and which has vigorously and rightly insisted upon the sole test of scholarship for membership on the faculty.

The answer to the question of who will teach also involves the practical consideration of the sources and availability of scholars in religion. Currently it appears that Biblical scholars, church historians, and scholars in various other aspects of theology are available in considerable number whereas scholars in such areas as history of religions and sociology and psychology of religion are in short supply. This condition exists in part because of the fact that most of the programs designed to produce qualified scholars in religion have been associated with theological faculties in seminaries and university divinity schools where there has been a primary interest in theological scholarship and related areas. The development of advanced programs in religion not directly related to professional theological faculties has been a relatively recent phenomenon in America. Thus many if not most of the men qualified to teach in religion have received much of their training under theological faculties.[13]

The fact that many of the available scholars in religion have received much of their education under theological faculties, together with the fact that most of these men are ordained clergymen, can be an additional complicating element in the sensitive atmosphere of a state university. Some academicians fear or suspect that men of this type of background cannot be as critical in their approach to their subject as the canons of the university would seem to demand. This sort of fear may be heightened in those instances in which the ordained clergyman is under some sort of direct and functioning ecclesiastical authority. Thus there might be some preference for the appointment of laymen, rather than clergymen, to teach in religion. But the supply of qualified lay scholars has been limited in the field of religion generally, and in theology in particular. Furthermore, it is not entirely evident that laymen have been or are necessarily more critical or more scholarly in their approach to religion than ordained clergymen.

Those responsible for the structuring of a curricular program in religion must inevitably make certain decisions about the issues discussed here and about the areas of the field to be developed, priorities in the development of these areas, and the manner in which the program will be fitted into the general curricular structure of the college or university. Some argue for the primacy of the study of the Western religious heritage on the ground that this is nearest to us and of most relevance to the students. In such instances, the emphasis might be upon Biblical studies, or the history of religion in the West, or the development of religious thought, or religion in America, or religion and contemporary issues. Others call for an emphasis upon the major religions of the world, assuming perhaps that students know something of their own religious heritage (an assumption that is not always well founded), and arguing that such a study affords a more thorough exposure to the nature and function of religion and also broadens the students' horizons. In a number of state universities where the question of studies in religion has been under consideration a preference has been expressed for the type of program that can be developed in connection with already existing departments. In such cases an effort might be made to appoint men with interest and scholarly competence in some aspect of religion to such departments as philosophy, sociology, and history. A few state universities have sought to build a curricular program in religion by utilizing qualified campus clergymen as teachers in the area. Others have endeavored to build and operate a department of religion in much the same manner in which other academic departments are structured. The accounts which follow describe programs of various types in which the various issues discussed here have been answered, explicitly or implicitly, in a variety of ways.

---

1. Andrew D. White's *A History of the Warfare of Science with Theology in Christendom* (1896) was a product of this atmosphere and illustrates a prevailing mood of the late nineteenth century. The publication of 1896 was based on a briefer treatment which first appeared in print as a pamphlet in 1876. White was the first president of Cornell University.

2. Professor George Ernest Wright refers to this period as "the golden age of Old Testament study." Developments in such other areas as church history, sociology of religion, psychology of religion, and history of religions were also of such a nature in this period as to warrant the designation for the whole field of religion. The quotation from Professor Wright is found in *Protestant Thought in the Twentieth Century*, Arnold S. Nash, ed. (New York, Macmillan Co., 1951), p. 20.

3. For a fuller treatment of historical detail, see Clyde A. Holbrook, *Religion, A Humanistic Field* (Englewood Cliffs, N.J., Prentice-Hall, Inc., 1963), Introduction;

Robert Michaelsen, "Religion in the Undergraduate Curriculum," in *The Making of Ministers*, Keith R. Bridston and Dwight W. Culver, eds. (Minneapolis, Augsburg Publishing House, 1964), pp. 43-71; and Robert Michaelsen, *The Scholarly Study of Religion in College and University* (New Haven, The Society for Religion in Higher Education, 1964), pp. 8-11.

4. For a survey of the increase of religion instruction and of developments in scholarship in this area see Holbrook, *op. cit.*, chaps. 4, 12. See also Gerhard Lenski, "Review of Theoretically Oriented Research," in *The Sociology of Religion in the United States* (rep. ser. No. 6, Center for Research in Social Organization, Department of Sociology, The University of Michigan, Ann Arbor, 1962) for developments in the sociology of religion; and *Readings in the Psychology of Religion*, Orlo Strunk, Jr., ed. (New York, Abingdon Press, 1959), esp. chap. I on "History," for developments in the psychology of religion. Developments in the history of religions are treated by Joachim Wach in *The Comparative Study of Religions*, J. M. Kitagawa, ed. (New York and London, Columbia University Press, 1958; Columbia paperback edition, 1961), chap. I, and by Mircea Eliade in "The History of Religions in Retrospect: 1912-1962," *The Journal of Bible and Religion*, XXXI (April, 1963), pp. 98-109.

The volume on *Religion* in the "Princeton Studies on Humanistic Scholarship in America" deals with developments in such areas as theology, philosophy of religion, history of religions, and Biblical studies. The general editor of the series is Richard Schlatter and the editor of the volume on religion is Paul Ramsey (Englewood Cliffs, N. J., Prentice-Hall, Inc., 1965).

McLean and Kimber (*op. cit.*) give some idea of developments in twenty-five state universities up to 1958.

The University of Wisconsin instituted its Ph.D. in Buddhist studies in its Indian Language and Area Center. Thus the specialized study of this major religious tradition has developed in connection with an area studies program.

An interesting recent development which has grown in part out of the increase of interest in theology is the appointment of scholars in Catholic studies at such institutions as Harvard, Yale, Stanford, Western Michigan, and the University of Iowa. Recent appointments in the area of Hebrew language and literature at such institutions as Yale, Indiana, and Wisconsin (both Madison and Milwaukee) also suggest an increase of interest in the study of Judaism.

5. Perhaps the most persuasive such arguments for the legitimacy of the scholarly study of religion in state universities have appeared in the statements of faculty committees charged with studying this question in various institutions. Some of these statements are cited in this study, including those made by committees at Michigan and Indiana. Others which have recently come to my attention include statements made by similar committees at the Universities of Illinois and Tennessee.

On the legal question see Robert C. Casad, "On Teaching Religion at the State University," *Kansas Law Review*, 12, March, 1964, pp. 405-416; Wilbur G. Katz, *Religion and American Constitutions* (Evanston, Northwestern University Press, 1964), esp. p. 50 ff.; Paul G. Kauper, "Law and Public Opinion," in *Religion and the State University*, Erich A. Walter, ed. (Ann Arbor, The University of Michigan Press, 1958; Ann Arbor Paperback, 1964), pp. 69-86; and "Schempp and Sherbert: Studies in Neutrality and Accommodation" in *Religion and the Public Order*, Donald A. Gianella, ed. (Chicago, The University of Chicago Press, 1964), pp. 3-40; David M. Louisell and John H. Jackson, "Religion, Theology, and Public Higher

Education," *California Law Review*, 50, December, 1962, pp. 751-799; and Robert Michaelsen, "The Supreme Court and Religion in Public Higher Education," *Journal of Public Law*, Emory University Law School, 13, No. 2, 1964, pp. 343-352.

6. See the chapter on Princeton (chap. IX, esp. fn. 1).

7. On the nature of religion as an academic field and for discussions of terminology and of trends in relevant disciplines and sub-disciplines see Holbrook, *op. cit.*, chaps. 2 and 3; Ramsey, *op. cit.*, and Michaelsen, *The Scholarly Study of Religion in College and University*, pp. 12-26. My treatment of the subject in this present context is largely a summary of that presented in the latter work.

8. The quotations are from Eliade, *op. cit.*, pp. 100-101; *Patterns of Comparative Religion*, translated from the French by Rosemary Sheed (London and New York, Sheed and Ward, 1958), p. xi; and "History of Religions and a New Humanism," *History of Religions*, I, Summer 1961, pp. 4-5. See also the relevant discussions of G. Van der Leeuw, Joachim Wach, W. C. Smith, Joseph M. Kitagawa and Philip H. Ashby. These are listed in Michaelsen, *op. cit.*, note 12, p. 33.

9. See, e.g., G. Van der Leeuw, *Religion in Essence and Manifestation* (New York and Evanston, Harper and Row, Harper Torchbook, 1963).

10. A suggestive list of works resulting from studies of this type can be found in Michaelsen, *op. cit.*, note 23, p. 34.

11. For a brief discussion of trends in contemporary theology, see Daniel Day Williams, *What Present-Day Theologians Are Thinking* (rev. ed., New York, Harper and Brothers, 1959), and Claude Welch's essay in the volume on *Religion* in the "Princeton Studies on Humanistic Scholarship," cited in fn. 4 above.

12. For presentations of these contrasting points of view within one volume see the essays by John Courtney Murray, S.J., Will Herberg and William Frankena in *Religion and the State University*, cited in fn. 5 above. See also Herman E. Wornom, "Critical Issues of Religion in Public Higher Education," in *Legal and Other Critical Issues of Religion in Public Higher Education;* (A Symposium published by the Religious Education Association, 545 West 111th St., New York, n.d.) and the chapter on "Sectarianism, Pluralism, and Tax-Supported Institutions" in Holbrook, *op. cit.*

13. On graduate education in religion see Holbrook, *op. cit.*, chap. 10.

I
AN INTERDEPARTMENTAL PROGRAM IN RELIGION:
The University of Michigan

Above the entrance to Angell Hall, the massive gray stone structure named for one of Michigan's most illustrious presidents, are carved the words from the Northwest Ordinance: "Religion, morality, and knowledge being necessary to good government and the happiness of mankind, schools and the means of education shall forever be encouraged."[1] Today there extends to the rear of Angell two relatively new brick structures, Haven and Mason Halls, one named for another Michigan president and the other for the man who was Governor of the state when the University was founded. Together these three buildings house many of the major departments in the College of Literature, Science and the Arts. Between them these departments contribute to the dissemination and advance of knowledge on a scale unthought of by the framers of the phrase which greets one as he enters Angell.

A close look at the College will reveal a breadth in curricular offerings and scholarly activities related in some way to the study of religion which is matched by few other state universities in the United States. Here one will find relevant and sometimes even exciting and distinguished work going on in such areas as Buddhist studies, Islamic civilization and philosophy, religious life and thought in the ancient Near East, and psychology, sociology, and philosophy of religion. Obvious provision for the systematic study of the major religions of the West—especially post-Biblical Judaism and Christianity—is, however, strangely lacking.

History and Rationale

The present curricular structure and program in religion at the University of Michigan is largely the result of the establishment and activities of the Special Administrative Committee on Studies in Religion in the College of Literature, Science and the Arts, the interests of existing departments in the study of religion, and the presence or lack of financial support. There is no department of religion at Michigan. The interdepartmental committee acts in lieu of a department but without departmental status or budget. This committee may encourage departments to offer relevant courses. In the final analysis, however, the offering of such courses is largely a departmental decision.

Financial support—either from internal or external sources—for the direct study of religion has been minimal. However, support of related areas has sometimes had the effect of increasing the study of religion. For example, the development of area studies programs in recent years, with support from foundations and the U. S. Government as well as from the University, has brought some increase in attention to such fields as Buddhism and Chinese and Indian philosophy and art.

There is a long history of interest in the study of religion at the University of Michigan. The first president, Henry W. Tappan, urged the religious groups of the state to establish seminaries or chairs of theology adjacent to the campus. Although this suggestion bore no fruit efforts were made to establish independent and non-denominational schools of religion in the early twentieth century. Two such schools were established and operated for brief periods of time—one in the early years of the century and the other in the 1920's. Neither managed to continue in existence, but funds raised in connection with the second school were turned over to the University for the support of public lectures and conferences on religion. A Counselor on Religious Education was appointed in 1933. Under his direction an interdepartmental degree program in religion and ethics was established in 1937.

In 1947 the Dean of the College of Literature, Science and the Arts appointed an *ad hoc* faculty committee to study academic offerings in religion in that College. The first committee report, submitted in 1948, expressed opposition to the establishment of a department of religion and recommended instead: (*a*) the inclusion of specialists in religion in various relevant departments; (*b*) the addition of two faculty members entirely concerned with teaching and research relating to religion —the departmental base of these men to be determined on the basis of their qualifications and research interests; and (*c*) the appointment of a standing faculty committee on religion with responsibility in this area analogous to that normally borne by a department, the chairman of the committee to be one of the men referred to in (*b*). The committee stressed the importance of courses of a general liberal arts nature open to all students in the College rather than the development of a program of specialization. However, it did recommend that an undergraduate degree program in religion be continued and that it be placed under the supervision of the standing committee. The *ad hoc* faculty committee urged the following courses as most desirable and essential: The History of Religion, "a two-semester course covering the main religions, living or dead, of the world"; Comparative Religion;

Great Religious Books, which the committee felt to be more desirable than the ordinary type introductory course in religion; the Bible, Old and New Testaments; The History of Christianity and Judaism; Religion in America; The Psychology of Religion; The Philosophy of Religion; The Sociology of Religion; and Primitive Religion. Finally, the committee expressed strong sentiments to the effect that courses in this area should be *about* religion, thus avoiding anything of a "dogmatic, missionary, proselyting, ceremonial, or inspirational" nature, and that while the personal religious position of the teacher was irrelevant to the academic concerns of the University, it should not be assumed that one who was sympathetic toward religion or committed to a particular religious position could not be qualified to teach in this area.[2]

Steps were taken to carry out these recommendations, especially in the restructuring of an interdepartmental major in religion, the appointment of a standing committee (the Special Administrative Committee on Studies in Religion), and the appointment of some faculty members with interests in religion in certain relevant departments. The first report of the Committee on Studies in Religion, submitted in 1956, reiterated the basic position of the 1948 report, reviewed progress to date, and pointed out that the course offerings of the College in the area of religion had been "left incomplete," and the A.B. program in Studies in Religion "without a center," and in general that the work of the College in this field had been "given no leader who was competent to spear-head it as a whole." Therefore, the Committee recommended the appointment "as soon as possible . . . of a full-time man in the field of the history and comparison of religions . . . ." The Committee also recommended that a clear line be drawn between religious activities—and specifically the work of Lane Hall, the center for religious activities—and the study of religion. In part in keeping with this recommendation the Committee asked for a budget which would enable it to bring to the campus noted speakers in the area of religion—a practice which had been carried on by Lane Hall.[3]

During the period between the issuance of the 1956 report and 1958, when the Committee made another report, funds were made available for visiting speakers in religion and an effort was made to find and appoint a full-time scholar in the history of religion. The interdepartmental major also continued in existence, being slightly altered as courses formerly offered ceased to be offered and as new courses were introduced. The 1958 report contains many of the same recommendations of the earlier reports, but with one significant change. The Committee apparently reached the conclusion that the appointment of a single individual in the history of religion was not as feasible as had earlier been thought to be the case. This might have been due, in part, to the difficulties in locating a scholar who was qualified for and would accept such an appointment. In any case, the 1958 report no longer called for such an appointment, but recommended instead that the Committee be granted the responsibility and resources necessary to develop and offer *a course* in the history of religion or comparative religion. The Committee reasoned that

the indefinable nature of religion, the complexity of its involvement with the whole of culture especially in many Asian religious traditions, and the tremendous demands in linguistic, philological, and historical training required for an adequate understanding of any one religion, all make it perfectly clear that no one person can possibly have the ideal competence required to give such a course.

Furthermore, the Committee expressed serious doubts about the adequacy of a comparative method in religion, "for it seems that to compare religions is to compare civilizations." Thus the Committee pointed to the necessity that a course in the history of religion be staffed by a group of scholars with specialties in various areas. The Committee also urged the desirability of graduate study in this area, pointing to the resources already present for such study at the University of Michigan, calling for additional appointments in such areas as early Christian history and thought (in the History Department), the New Testament and related literatures (in Classical Studies), Near Eastern history in the Hellenistic-Roman period with a concentration on post-Biblical Judaism (in Near Eastern Studies), and medieval religious philosophy and modern religious thought (in the Philosophy Department), and concluding that research and graduate concentration in this area would of necessity need to involve an interdepartmental approach.

The 1958 report called for support for additional teaching staff, for releasing time of faculty members in relevant areas in order that they might work on the history of religion course and/or engage in research in this area, and for visiting lecturers, additions to the library, graduate fellowships and scholarships, and relevant publications. The Committee estimated that approximately $400,000 would be needed over a five-year period to carry out its recommendations.[4]

As of the Summer of 1964 no further Committee reports had been issued and most of the recommendations of the 1958 report were still "on the drawing board." However, the course in history of religion or comparative religion, recommended in the 1958 report, was offered for the first time during the 1963-64 academic year as a non-departmental course in the honors program and under the title, "The Nature of Religion." This course was developed as a "pilot course" by two members of the Department of Near Eastern Languages and Literature. The course was being taught by one of these men whose work in this connection was augmented by a small grant from the Danforth Foundation.

During the 1963-64 academic year the curricular program in religion was studied by a commission which was University-wide in nature and which was appointed by the Vice President for Academic Affairs. The Commission on Studies in Religion in The Curriculum of the University of Michigan was created in part in response to a resolution presented by the Board of Governors for Religious Affairs. The Board recommended that the objectives of the Commission should be:

(1) To consider the responsibility of the University for courses depicting the history, art and philosophy of religious movements, for courses portraying contemporary religious thought and theology, and for courses considering the interaction of religious values with current developments in the areas of social, biological and physical sciences, and for courses including a treatment of ethics in vocational practice.

(2) To review the present curricular offerings in these areas.

(3) To consider procedures by which needed courses may be sponsored and supported, particularly when they may not fall within the established programs and budgets of the departments of the University.

(4) To investigate non-University sources of support for experimental programs arising under point (1).

(5) To consider the relation of the proposed Center for Theological Studies in Southeastern Michigan (sponsored by the Greater Detroit Study Commission on Theological Education) to the University.

(6) To make recommendations on these matters for action by the University administration and staff.[5]

The Commission on Studies in Religion in The Curriculum of the University of Michigan issued its Report in June of 1964. The Commission urged that the University is free to and should study religion "both as a specific phenomenon and as it interacts with the totality of human culture." Recognizing that the University of Michigan "does

study religion," and that "the range of religious phenomena dealt
with in courses now offered . . . is quite extensive," the Commission
concluded, however, that what is being done is inadequate to the
subject, considering the nature and responsibility of the University
for the study of religion. The Commission found existing offerings
inadequate at two points: (1) in the relatively small amount of attention given to the religious traditions of most significance in our own
culture; and (2) in dealing with the interrelationships between religion and various aspects of culture, such as law, politics and social
structure, the arts, and language, literature and philosophy. The University has not fully exercised its freedom to study religion in such
a manner that religion receives "the same scholarly treatment accorded
a wide diversity of academic fields. Moreover, the religions it studies
most adequately are not the ones most influential in the formation of
the country's culture." Furthermore, the Commission pointed out,
"the treatment of particular religious phenomena within the framework of modern academic disciplines may easily have nothing to do
at all with religion *per se.*" For example, the academic study of
religious art might be "concerned only with the development of artistic style, technique, and aesthetic taste" and give little or no attention
to the "religious concerns which motivated and gave religious significance to those works of art. . . ." And the Commission noted that
similar examples might be drawn from such fields as "philosophy and
history, literature and music."

Specifically, the Commission concluded that "the most crucially
important fields now lacking specialists are the following:

a. The New Testament and related literatures, especially early
   Christian.
b. The Talmud and subsequent post-Biblical Jewish literature and
   history.
c. The History of Christian Thought, including the Protestant
   Reformation.
d. Contemporary religious thought: theologies since 1850.
e. Hindu literature and religious thought."

In order to help eliminate the "serious deficiencies" which exist the
Commission recommended (1) that the recommendations made by the
Committee on Studies in Religion presented to the Dean of the College of Literature, Science, and the Arts in December, 1958 (referred
to above), be more fully implemented; and (2) that the University
establish "an institute for the advanced study of religion." Such an
institute, which the Commission regarded as its "most important

recommendation," would have three major functions: "(1) to carry out research; (2) to assist in curriculum planning and development; and (3) to serve as a liaison agency both among divisions and departments within the University and between the University and organizations external to the University." On "the graduate level and higher, it would strive to create new knowledge through research." On the undergraduate level, "it would present orderly knowledge of the religious traditions which inform our own culture."

The staff of the proposed institute would be made up of an administrative director, faculty members in the University "whose field of specialization concerns some aspect of the study of religion," and visiting scholars. The Commission estimated that $150,000 a year would be needed for salaries of the director and visiting scholar, support of research both independent and through an interdisciplinary seminar, fellowships both post-doctoral and graduate, library, and administrative expenses.[6]

The Commission's Report was made to the Vice President for Academic Affairs and is now in the hands of the University administration.

Curriculum and Selected Courses

While the Committee on Studies in Religion of the College of Literature, Science and the Arts has not regarded the concentration program in religion as its major concern, this program has been in operation for over a decade and it is one of the more obvious aspects of the Committee's work, since information about the program appears in the catalogue of the College. The number of majors in religion has not been large. It has ranged from two to three in the mid-1950's to as many as ten in the early 1960's. The establishment of the program has, however, accomplished more than making it possible for a student to major in religion. It has enabled the Committee to spell out what it has considered necessary to a concentration in religion, to list together courses in relevant areas, and to encourage departments to add other courses. The listing of the Studies in Religion program in the catalogue has also served to call attention of students to courses in this area, whether they might be interested in majoring or not.

The concentration program in religion requires 35 hours distributed as follows:

A. Three courses are required "as fundamental disciplines necessary for an adequate understanding of religion":

Psychology and Religion (offered by the Psychology Department)

Problems of Religion (offered by the Philosophy Department)
Religion and Society (offered by the Sociology Department)

B. At least nine hours from the following courses, including one
two-semester sequence:

Primitive Religion (Anthropology)

Greek Mythology; Greek Religion; Greeks, Romans, and Egyptians (Classical Studies)

History of Far Eastern Thought; Brahmanism and Hinduism; Buddhism; Confucianism; Readings in Chinese Thought (East Asian Thought)

Intellectual History of Medieval Europe; Western Europe from 1500 to 1618 (History)

Historical Background of the Bible; Muslim Religious Philosophy; History of Ancient Religions; Social and Religious Thought of the Hebrew Prophets; The Formation of Islamic Civilization; and The Near East in the Period of the Crusades (Near Eastern Studies)

C. A minimum of 18 hours in one of the following departments:

Religion as idea—Philosophy

Religion as a cultural force through time—History

Religion as individual experience and behavior—Psychology

Religion as a social phenomenon and behavior—Sociology or Cultural Anthropology

Religion as the subject of expression—English Literature, or History of Art

Religious traditions—Near East, including Hebrew or Arabic; Classics, including Greek or Latin; Far Eastern, including Chinese or Japanese

D. A number of other courses are strongly recommended, including such courses as The Gospels of Mark and Matthew (Greek); Early Christian Art and Archaeology; Milton; The English Bible: Its Literary Aspects and Influence; Major English Authors of the Renaissance; Chinese Literature in English; Japan's Literary Heritage; Church and State in Anglo-American Society (History); Art of India; Art of China; Buddhist Art; Early Christian Art; The Indian Temple (History of Art); Music in History; and relevant courses in Philosophy.[7]

Enrollments in selected courses dealing directly with religion are listed for recent academic years in Table I. These figures indicate that

TABLE I

Enrollments in Selected Courses Dealing with Religion:
University of Michigan*

Course	1955-56		1957-58		1960-61		1961-62		1962-63		1963-64	
	I	II	I	II	I	II	I	II	I	II	I	II
Psychology and Religion (Psych.)	107		84		107		68		65		35	
Problems of Religion (Philos.)	112		72		69		81		72		74	
Religion and Society (Sociol.)	27		56				63		91			
Greek Religion (Classics)							11					
Primitive Religion (Anthropology)			26				29		29			
Brahmanism and Hinduism (Far East)						9						
Buddhism (Far East)	7		6		12		18		17		25	
Confucianism (Far East; Philosophy)						3		7				11
Asian Philosophy (Philos.)												23
History of Far Eastern Thought (Far East)	13	12	18	20	18	20	34	34	22	19	14	20
Historical Background of Bible (Near East)			59	48	49	99			54	62		
Muslim Religious Philosophy (Near East; Philos.)	8		3				14					
Formation of Islamic Civilization (Near East)									32		24	
Philosophy of Religion (Philos.)				10						21		9
English Bible (English)	88		88	100	40	59	41	50	50	49		50
Nature of Religion (Honors)†											27	25
Social and Religious Thought of Hebrew Prophets (Near East; Philos.)‡												
History of Ancient Religions (Near East)§												

* The figures include only those registered for credit. The parentheses indicate the department. Course numbers have varied from year to year. Figures supplied by Mrs. Ruth A. Brown, Statistician, College of Literature, Science and the Arts, the University of Michigan.

† First offered, Fall, 1963. Enrollment limited.

‡ Offered once in the last ten years: 1959-60 (II); enrollment, 40.

§ Listed but not offered as of Fall, 1963.

the courses which have been most consistently offered are Psychology and Religion; Problems of Religion; Religion and Society; Buddhism; Historical Background of the Bible; History of Far Eastern Thought; and The English Bible. Four of these are described here:

(1) Psychology and Religion is a two-semester hour course which has been developed chiefly by Professor Wilbert J. McKeatchie of the Psychology Department. The course, which requires "Introduction to Psychology as a Natural Science," or "Introduction to Psychology as a Social Science," or equivalent, or senior standing as a prerequisite, deals with "psychological processes in religious phenomena and as an interpretation of the psychological meaning of religion." Thirteen lectures were delivered in the course by various members of the Psychology Department in the Spring of 1963 on such topics as the relationship between science and religion; conflicts between psychology and religion; the nature of thought; the nature of man as seen by theology; the nature of man as seen by social psychology; religion, economics and personality; sources of morality and guilt; cognition, motivation, belief, and behavior; religious conversion and transference; and rituals. Assigned readings included selections from the following: *What, Then, Is Man?* (A Symposium of Theology, Psychology, and Psychiatry, developed by The School of Graduate Studies of Concordia Theological Seminary) ; Adorno *et al., The Authoritarian Personality;* Rokeach, *The Open and Closed Mind;* Beach and Niebuhr, *Christian Ethics* (Selection from Rauschenbusch); Riesman *et al., The Lonely Crowd;* Miller and Swanson, *Changing American Parent;* Herberg, *Protestant, Catholic, Jew;* Newcomb, *Readings in Social Psychology;* Cooley, *Social Organization;* McClelland, *Studies in Motivation;* Allport, *Becoming;* Fromm, *Man For Himself;* and the Skinner contribution to Dulany *et al., Contributions to Modern Psychology.*[8]

Psychology and Religion was considerably revised before the Spring of 1964 and was taught by a doctoral candidate in the Psychology Department. The outline for the Spring semester of 1964 was as follows:

I. Introduction
    A. The Nature of Psychology: Three Forces
        1. Freudian and orthodox psychoanalysis
        2. Experimental-positivistic-behavioristic theories
        3. The "Third Force"
    B. The Nature of Religion: The Problem of Definition

C. Conflict between Psychology and Religion
D. Psychology and Religion: Scope and History

II. Psychological Theories of Religion
A. William James
B. James H. Leuba
C. Sigmund Freud and Other Orthodox Psychoanalytic Statements
D. C. G. Jung
E. Gordon W. Allport
F. Erich Fromm
G. Behaviorism: B. F. Skinner and William Sargant

III. Problems of Methodology

IV. Religion in the Developing Personality

V. The Religious Life
A. Conversion
B. Mysticism
C. Worship
D. Prayer

VI. Religion and Mental Health
A. Psychopathology and Religion
B. Faith Healing
C. Psychotherapy versus Spiritual Counseling

VII. Fringes and Frontiers

VIII. Overview

(2) Problems of Religion is an upper level four-semester hour course open to students who have had an introductory course in philosophy. It is described as "a philosophic examination of basic religious problems such as the nature of religion, the existence and nature of God, methods of attaining religious knowledge, the problem of evil, and immortality." The texts used in the fall semester, 1963-64, were William P. Alston, *Religious Belief and Philosophical Thought* and John Hick, *Philosophy of Religion.*

(3) Religion and Society is a three-semester hour course with a prerequisite of an introductory course in sociology or the permission of the instructor. It is described as "an analysis of religious institutions and of their interrelations with economic, political, and other societal institutions," with special attention being given to the religions of the Western world. When taught in the Spring of 1963 (by Professor

Gerhard Lenski, who has since left the University of Michigan) the course concentrated on three basic problem areas in the sociology of religion, set in a historical framework: (1) origins or sources of religious beliefs; (2) the nature of religious organizations; and (3) influences of religion on the social life. Special attention was given to religion in American society in the last third of the course.

(4) The English Bible; Its Literary Aspects and Influence, is a two-semester course, two hours each semester, which has been offered quite consistently over the past several years and which has had enrollments varying from 40 to 100. The course is listed as a 400 course—upper level—but there are no prerequisites. The Old Testament, excepting the Prophets, is the point of focus in the Fall semester, and the New Testament and the Prophets form the content for the Spring semester. The only textbook is the Bible. A paperback handbook—such as an introduction to the Bible or one dealing with the history of Biblical literature—is recommended for the students' own use. While the literary influence of the Bible is stressed, the chief goal of the course is an intensive exposure of the student to the Bible itself—in English translation. Attention is devoted to history, to archaeological backgrounds, etc., only to the extent needed in helping to gain an understanding and appreciation of the passages being read. The lectures supply such introductory material as date of composition, writing, authorship, circumstances under which the book came into being, audience for which it was intended, outline of contents, and summary evaluation as a work of literature. The approach is much the same as that employed in any other course in literature.

The Nature of Religion, introduced in the Fall of 1963 for students in the Honors Program in the College of Literature, Science, and the Arts, is a full year course offered for three semester hours each semester. During the first semester of 1963-64 the course consisted of an examination of the following items, among others: the religious community, the system of communication, the constitutive, the functional, and the historical factors in religion. Illustrations were drawn from a broad variety of sources including primitive, Eastern and ancient Near Eastern religions. The texts included Levy, *Religious Conceptions of the Stone Age; Ancient Religions,* Ferm, ed.; Enslin, *Christian Beginnings* and *Literature of the Christian Movement; Islam* (Selected Texts), Jeffrey, ed.; Sen, *Hinduism;* Conze, *Buddhism, Its Essence and Development* and *Buddhist Scriptures;* Bruce, *Religions in Japan;* and van Gennep, *The Rites of Passage.* Students were also given an extensive bibliography upon which to draw in engaging in their own studies. As a "pilot course," enrollment was restricted to twenty-seven students from the honors program, although considerably more than this number were interested in taking the course. It was anticipated that the course might be continued another year and opened to other students as well as those in the Honors Program.

Courses in the Far Eastern area, such as Buddhism, Brahmanism and Hinduism, and Confucianism, have been offered only in recent years. The establishment of such courses has resulted largely from foundation, governmental and University support of area studies. Such support may make possible the introduction of additional courses in such areas as Chinese and Indian philosophy. This points to the rather striking fact that the study of religion may be approached un- abashedly when dealing with non-Western areas in which religion has played such a dominating role while the study of religion in the West is a fragmentary affair handled indirectly by various departments whose primary concern is with other subjects. Thus courses in Buddhism or Hinduism or Confucianism may be freely accepted as being essential to an area studies program whereas courses in Chris- tianity or Judaism find no such favorable environment. It is possible that the recognition of the validity of the direct study of Buddhism, for example as a major religious tradition with its various literatures and philosophies, with its inner life and its influence upon societies and civilizations, may bring a similar recognition of the validity of the direct study of Christianity or Judaism. Such does not seem likely, however, because of the patterns of current departmental structure, a traditional academic bias against the direct study of major Western religious traditions, and the patent lack of funds. Furthermore, even the area study programs have developed in such a manner that studies in religious traditions, and humanistic studies generally, have played a relatively minor role.

Conclusions

It is obvious that the study of religion is going on at the University of Michigan, both in the classroom and in the research of scholars. The Committee on Studies in Religion has endeavored to give form and order to this study. It has sought to develop an interdepartmental program which would build upon the richness of curricular offering and scholarly work already taking place by encouraging the addition of courses in relevant areas and of qualified scholars to existing departments. The course on The Nature of Religion shows promise of becoming a significant and even popular offering in the College of Literature, Science, and the Arts—if it receives sufficient financial support and is granted some sort of structural home.

But after a study of the Interdepartmental Program in Religion one cannot avoid the conclusion that it does not measure up to the stature of the University of Michigan. The major religious traditions of the West have received little systematic scholarly attention in the curriculum—as the Commission on Studies in Religion in the Curriculum of the University of Michigan recognized. Research in religion has not kept pace with research in a host of other areas. And despite the work of the members of the committees and commissions concerned with the study of religion, the program in religion has lacked a vital functioning core.

Michigan's experience of more than fifteen years would appear to indicate that an interdepartmental program supervised by a faculty committee can encounter two problems of sizeable proportions: (1) where to fit into the structure of existing academic departments the scholar concerned with the direct study of religion—such as the scholar in comparative religion or history of religions (*Religionswissenschaft*), or the theologian; and (2) who will "mind the store," i.e., do those administrative jobs having to do with budget, hiring, promotion, acquisition of library materials, etc., which can be so essential to the welfare of any academic program. Disciplines devoted to the direct study of religion, such as the history of religions and theology, have not flourished at Michigan. Nearly all curricular offerings have been left to the discretion of existing departments, and quantity and quality of offerings have varied with the varying interests and enthusiasms of these departments and of the faculty within them. No single individual or group has had the power or the budget to coordinate curricular offerings or to encourage relevant research. In an atmosphere where the competition for funds grows stiffer, such an interdepartmental program is in danger of being left behind for lack of administrative and faculty energies and financial support.

An institute for the advanced study of religion, such as the one proposed by the Commission on Studies in Religion, might become the kind of administrative core or academic center which could attract distinguished scholars in religion, stimulate research, and promote the enhancement of offerings in religion in the undergraduate curriculum.

*Selected Biographical and Bibliographical Information About
Selected Senior Faculty Who Teach Courses Related
to Religion—1963-64*

ALSTON, WILLIAM P. (Philosophy).

B. 1921; Centenary College, B.M. 1942; Chicago, Ph.D. 1951; teaching at Michigan, 1951-.

Interests: Philosophy of religion, philosophy of language, metaphysics in relationship to the new philosophy.

Publications: Religious Belief and Philosophical Thought, 1963; *Readings in Twentieth-Century Philosophy* (with G. Nakhnikian), 1962; numerous articles.

HOURANI, GEORGE F. (Near Eastern Studies and Philosophy).

B. 1913; Oxford, B.A. 1936; Princeton, Ph.D. 1939; teaching at Michigan, 1950-.

Interests: Ancient Near and Far Eastern philosophy, especially Muslim and Indian thought.

Publications: Numerous articles and reviews.

LINK, ARTHUR E. (Far Eastern Studies).

B. 1920; California, B.A. 1947, M.A. 1948, Ph.D. 1957; teaching at Michigan, 1957-1964.

Interests: Chinese language, literature, religion and philosophy; Indian and Central Asian Buddhism.

Publications: Numerous articles.

MCKEATCHIE, WILBERT J. (Psychology).

B. 1921; Michigan State Normal, B.A. 1952; Michigan, Ph.D. 1949; teaching at Michigan, 1948-.

Interests: Interaction of social and psychological and personal factors, psychology of teaching and learning.

Publications: Motivation, Teaching Methods and College Learning (Nebraska Symposium on Motivation, 1961). Numerous articles and reviews.

MENDENHALL, GEORGE E. (Near Eastern Studies).

B. 1916; Midland, B.A. 1936; Lutheran Seminary, Gettysburg, B.D. 1938; Johns Hopkins, Ph.D. 1947; teaching at Michigan, 1952-.

Interests: West-Semitic languages and literature, ancient Semitic religions; cultural history of Palestine and Syria in two millennia.

Publications: Law and Covenant in Israel and the Ancient Near East (Biblical Colloquium). Numerous monographs and articles.

STEVENS, ALBERT K. (English).

B. 1901; Calvin College, B.A. 1924; Michigan, M.A. 1926, Ph.D. 1949; teaching at Michigan, 1949-.

Interests: Theology and literary criticism in the nineteenth century; Milton and Chartism.

Publications: Numerous articles

---

1. This sentence is also found in the Michigan Constitution of 1909, Art. XI, Sect. 1.

2. "Report of the Committee on Religion," 1948, William Frankena, Chairman.

3. "Report of the Committee on Religion," March, 1956, William Frankena, Chairman.

4. "Report of the Committee on Studies in Religion," December, 1958, George Mendenhall, Chairman.

5. "Resolution" by the Board of Governors for Religious Affairs. This Board is appointed by the Board of Regents of the University of Michigan. It is made up of seven tenured faculty members, two alumni, two students and several ex-officios, including the Co-ordinator of Religious Affairs, the Chairman of the Committee on Studies in Religion, the President of the Association of Religious Counselors, the President of the Student Religious Association, and the Vice President for Student Affairs.

6. "Report of the Commission on Studies in Religion in the Curriculum of The University of Michigan," June 16, 1964, William J. Schlatter, Chairman.

7. From *The University of Michigan Official Publication, College of Literature, Science, and the Arts,* 1963-1964, pp. 266-268.

8. Course descriptions taken from *The University of Michigan Official Publication, College of Literature, Science, and the Arts,* 1963-64, and from course outlines and syllabi.

II

A DEPARTMENT OF RELIGION STAFFED BY SELECTED CAMPUS CLERGYMEN AND UNIVERSITY FACULTY:

Michigan State University

Many contrasts are evident as one moves from Ann Arbor to East Lansing, from the University of Michigan to Michigan State University. The manner in which the subject of religion is approached academically by these two institutions is no exception; in fact one could scarcely find more dissimilar approaches. The two institutions differ markedly in structure and rationale for handling the subject of religion, in pattern of major or concentration in this area, in complexion of faculty, and in size and type of student enrollment in courses in religion.

The Department of Religion at Michigan State University is built upon a frank recognition of religious pluralism and is staffed by selected campus clergymen and by some teachers with professorial status. Introductory courses are offered in America's three major faiths —Judaism, Roman Catholicism, and Protestantism. These courses are taught by clergymen who have the status of lecturers but are not paid by the University. Most of the other courses offered by the Department also deal with aspects of Judaism and Christianity and are taught by men of professorial rank. In 1963-64 one of these was assigned full time to the Department, two were shared with the Humanities program in the University College, one was retired from the Department of Foreign Studies and had an active part-time appointment in the Department of Religion for two terms, and one served both as Chairman of the Department of Religion and Associate Dean of the University College. Among them, these campus clergymen and teachers of professorial rank have offered as many as twenty-eight courses in a single year with enrollments in recent years ranging between 1,700 and 2,000 (cumulative for three terms or quarters). Most of the students who have taken these courses have been undergraduates who have had no previous work in religion and who have been majoring in some other area. The courses in religion at Michigan State have been, then, primarily service courses for undergraduates—although a major was instituted recently and a few graduate students have enrolled in this area.

History and Rationale

The Department of Religion at Michigan State owes its existence and present status largely to one man, Dr. Harry H. Kimber, Chairman of the Department since its origin in the late 1940's. Dr. Kimber joined the staff of Michigan State College as a professor of history more than three decades ago. With the internal reorganization of the College after World War II he became Director of the Division of Social Sciences in the College of Science and Arts. At that time some campus clergymen taught courses in religion but there was neither a departmental structure nor regularized administrative procedures for the selection of teachers or courses. As Director of the Division of Social Sciences, Dr. Kimber managed to bring about the establishment of a Department of Religion and to develop a curricular program by co-opting qualified faculty from other departments or fields and by pressing into service campus clergymen with sufficient qualifications to teach at the undergraduate level.

Course offerings, especially those dealing with the three major faiths, proved to be quite popular. The staff of the Department was gradually expanded as more campus clergymen were involved in the teaching program and as funds were made available for the appointment of a full-time faculty member in 1957. Today the Department appears to be quite well established in the College of Arts and Letters. A major in religion was proposed and approved by the College in the Spring of 1963. Graduate level work is offered and religion is acceptable as a minor in the graduate degree program of two or three departments. Student interest in courses in religion is considerable, and faculty advisors appear generally to be either favorably disposed toward these courses or noncommittal. A selected group of faculty members from other departments than Religion agreed that the atmosphere in 1963 was more friendly toward the study of religion than it had been a decade earlier.

Curricular offerings in religion at Michigan State are concerned primarily with "the essential teachings, beliefs, ethical outlooks, and religious practices of the major religious traditions."[1] The orientation of the Department is clearly toward the major religions of the West. All of the introductory courses deal with aspects of Judaism or Christianity and most of the other courses are concerned in one way or another with aspects of the Western religious heritage. To a considerable extent, the rationale appears to be one of beginning with the student in his own religious and theological context and seeking to ground him more thoroughly in that context. Furthermore, there appears to be an inherent assumption that this can best be done, at the elementary level at least, by teachers who are themselves adherents of and ordained clergymen in the particular faiths being studied. At the same time, however, men of professorial rank appear to be chosen primarily on the basis of academic competence and without formal regard for religious affiliations or ordination status. And it is these men who teach the higher numbered courses in religion.

Present Structure and Status[2]

A total of seven elementary courses, dealing with aspects of Judaism, Roman Catholicism, or Protestantism, were offered by selected campus clergymen in 1963-64. Three of these were listed under the heading "Introduction to Religion," and were described as being introductory surveys, one to "the principal teachings of the Christian religion, presented from the Protestant point of view," one to "the principal teachings of the Christian religion, presented from the Roman Catholic point of view," and the third as a "survey of the principal teachings of Judaism." These were two-quarter hour courses, the first two being offered each quarter and the Jewish course being offered two out of the three quarters. Enrollments in these courses have consistently been among the highest of the courses offered in the Department at Michigan State. (See Table II.) The Protestant course was offered in four different sections in each quarter during 1963-64, each section being taught by a different Protestant clergyman. A common text was Forell, *The Protestant Faith.* The other two courses were each offered in one section. The texts used in these courses were Linden and Costello, *Fundamentals of Religion,* in the Catholic course and Steinberg, *Basic Judaism,* in the Jewish course.

Of the four other courses taught by campus clergymen, two were offered by a Catholic priest and two by a Jewish rabbi. Christian Theology and Introduction to Christian Ethics, taught by the priest, have both consistently had high enrollments. Enrollments in Jewish Institutions and Movements and in Hebrew Prophets have varied from 16 to 77 in recent years.

All other courses offered in the Department were taught by men with professorial rank. These courses ranged from Introduction to Christianity to The Protestant Reformation, and included such offerings as Old Testament, New Testament, Life of Christ, Writings of Paul, Eastern Christianity, Christian Ethics, Christian Thought, Classics of Christian Literature, Religion in American Culture, Religion and the Social Order, Comparative Religion, and Religious

Table II

Enrollments in Courses in Religion:*
Michigan State University

Course	1956-57	1958-59	1960-61	1961-62	1962-63	1963-64
101 Intro. Religion (Protestant)†..	498	332	354	361	544	576
105 Intro. Religion (R. Catholic)†	347	326	267	222	253	402
110 Intro. Religion (Jewish)‡	41	60	90	81	93	93
106 Christian Theology (RC)†	93	101	165	100	153	100
107 Christian Ethics (RC)†	102	110	109	131	149	55
111 Jewish Institutions and Movements§	59	16	49	31	32	14
112 Hebrew Prophets§	77	22	36	28	28	19
215 Intro. Christianity†	289	245	227	238	233	226
220 Old Testament§		17	15	25	29	32
221 Old Testament§		14	12	17	25	22
222 New Testament§		13	15	19	45	38
300 Life of Christ§	47	51	74	43	55	47
302 Writings of St. Paul§	36	18	23	30	46	29
315 Eastern Christianity§	16	14	11	13	23	19
400 Christian Ethics‡	100	54	30	47	46	36
400H Honors Work†			19	28	14	12
404 Christian Thought§	27	15	21	30	30	9
405 Christian Thought§	21	21	25	45	23	16
410 Religion in American Culture§			22	34	32	35
421 Religion and the Social Order§	11	14	21			
430 Classics of Christian Literature§	11		12	16	15	10
435 Comparative Religion§	25	47	36	46	52	41
436 Comparative Religion§	34	45	50	50	54	37
437 Religious Trends in Far East§				9	39	14
451 Protestant Reformation§	16	18	17	27	32	15
452 Protestant Reformation§	20	15	19	16	16	10
801 Graduate Reading†				6	2	9
Totals in Courses in Department of Religion	1,870	1,568	1,719	1,693	2,063	1,916
355 Philosophy of Religion (Philos.)§			45	58	94	103
464 Religion, Culture and Society (Sociol.)§			37		67	

* Michigan State University uses a three-quarter system; hence these figures represent cumulative enrollments for two- and three-term courses and are higher than figures for universities on a two-semester plan. Numbers of courses and course descriptions have varied considerably in the years covered by this Table. Numbers given here are those in the 1964-65 catalogue statement. The course enrollment figures were supplied by the Department of Religion, Harry H. Kimber, Chairman.

† 3 terms.   ‡ 2 terms.   § 1 term.

Trends in the Far East. About one-third of them were freshman-sophomore level and two-thirds junior-senior level. In general, there were no prerequisites for admission to any of the courses other than class status. It was possible for students to take a full year sequence in Biblical studies (two terms in Old Testament, the first being a prerequisite for admission to the second, and one term in New Testament), a full year sequence in Christian Thought—largely historical, a two-term sequence in Comparative Religion (one term dealing with major non-Western religions and the other being a comparative study of Judaism and Christianity), and a full year sequence in The Protestant Reformation. In addition, variable credit work was offered for Honors students and at the graduate level. Enrollment in all courses taught by men of professorial rank constituted about 30 per cent of the total enrollment in courses in the Department in 1956-57 and about 40 per cent in 1963-64.

Introduction to Christianity, a three-quarter hour course offered each quarter, was a somewhat more thorough study than the Protestant or Catholic sections of Introduction to Religion. Credit could not be received for both Introduction to Christianity and Introduction to Religion 101, which is the Protestant division of that course. The texts in use in Introduction to Christianity in the Fall of 1963 were Adam, *Spirit of Catholicism,* Richardson, *Theological Word Book of the Bible,* and Hordern, *A Layman's Guide to Protestant Theology.* The course enrolled an average of 75 students per quarter during the 1963-64 academic year.

The texts in use in selected other courses in the Fall of 1963 included Anderson, *Understanding the Old Testament;* Beck, *Through the Gospels to Jesus;* Gardner, *Biblical Faith and Social Ethics;* McGiffert-Cushman, *History of Christian Thought;* Olmstead, *Religion in America;* Herberg, *Protestant-Catholic-Jew;* Brown and Weigel, *An American Dialogue;* and Noss, *Man's Religions.* Syllabi and additional readings were also used in most of the courses beyond the introductory level.

The departmental requirements indicate that a candidate for the bachelor's degree in religion is required to take not fewer than 40-nor more than 70-quarter hours in religion, of which 24 must be in upper-class courses. Specific courses required for the major include Introduction to Christianity, the year sequence in Biblical studies, the year sequence in Christian Thought, and the term of Comparative Religion that deals with the religions of ancient Egypt, Greece, Rome, and those of India, China, Japan, and Persia. In addition 18 hours are required in specified allied subjects, to be selected from a list of relevant courses in Greek, Latin, music, sociology, philosophy, and history. The Department also specifies that Greek "will ordinarily be used to satisfy the language requirement of the College." The major in religion was authorized by the faculty in the Spring of 1963. Figures were not available on the number of students who had chosen this major since that date.

However, as indicated above, nearly all students who take courses in religion at Michigan State are undergraduate non-majors. An indication of the breadth of interest and areas of concentration of students enrolled in religion can be seen in the following breakdown of enrollment figures for 1962-63: 388 no major preference designated, 50 enrollments from Agriculture, 132 from Business and Public Service, 27 from Engineering, 78 from Home Economics, etc. It is also of interest to note that a number of students from the Honors College have been enrolled in religion courses.

Grading practices do not vary significantly from those of other departments. Grade averages by departments for the Spring of 1963 were as follows: comparative literature, 2.64; philosophy, 2.49; history, 2.34; English, 2.51; and religion, 2.69. The average for the College of Arts and Letters as a whole was 2.63 and the over-all University average was 2.56. So far as could be determined the courses in religion did not have a reputation for being "snap" courses. In fact, the Chairman expressed some concern that some of the instructors in Introduction to Religion 101, the Protestant course, were actually requiring too much work for an elementary level two-quarter hour course.

The curricular program in religion at Michigan State is obviously in a process of expansion. The first full-time teacher was appointed to the Department of Religion in 1957 and a second full-time teacher was added to the Religion faculty in the Fall of 1964. The Department will probably continue to use campus clergymen in the introductory courses where they teach now. The Chairman did indicate the desirability that a full-time faculty member might become co-ordinator of Introduction to Religion 101, the Protestant course. A common textbook and common requirements are already employed in this multiple section course, but further co-ordination under a man of professorial status might be helpful. There are indications that the religion major may attract a number of students and that graduate work may become more substantial and extensive in the future—possibly leading eventually to M.A. and Ph.D. programs in religion.

Conclusions

Working with the proverbial "shoe string," Professor Kimber has managed to develop a Department with a series of courses ranging from the elementary introductory courses on the three major religious traditions of America to relatively more advanced courses such as Religion in American Culture, Comparative Religion, and The Protestant Reformation, and with both a major and graduate study available. Enrollments are high and quite obviously the courses in religion are popular with students. In fact, the greatest strength of the program would appear to be its appeal to undergraduates.

The outside observer might be inclined to conclude that the development of this Department has been characterized by a fair amount of improvisation. The fact that the teaching staff of the Department is made up of campus clergymen who do not have professorial rank and of men of professorial status, three or four of whom also have responsibilities in other areas, could give rise to this sort of impression. It appears, however, that such a notable feature as the offering of "faith courses" by campus clergymen has not resulted solely from necessity or opportunism but has expressed a certain rationale—namely, that students should have an opportunity to study their own religious positions under clergymen representing those positions. Even if one accepted this position he might still ask why such courses should be taught by clergymen who are not trained primarily to teach religion at the university level, who are not producing scholars in the field of religion, and whose primary work and responsibility lie outside the university. Such an arrangement might appear to be more one of convenience than one in keeping with academic or scholarly criteria. However, it should be noted that, given an accepted policy of using campus clergymen as part-time instructors to teach introductory courses in their own religious traditions—debatable as this is—, Michigan State has shown some wisdom in the manner in which this policy has been carried out. Teachers are chosen carefully by the Chairman of the Department and courses are partially under departmental control. In other words, the University exercises about as much control and direction as it can under the circumstances. This practice stands in considerable contrast to that which existed prior to the establishment of the Department of Religion when little formal direction or co-ordination was provided by the College. It should also be noted that the academic caliber of some of the campus clergymen who have taught as lecturers in recent years has been high, as evidenced, for example, in the fact that several have gone on to responsible educational positions elsewhere: three to seminary professorships; one to a deanship; and one to an executive position in a national denominational organization. Moreover, these five men all held earned doctorates. In recent years the Department has endeavored to strengthen its staff through involving more men of professorial rank in its teaching program. This has tended to minimize somewhat the role of the campus clergymen teaching in the Department. The majority of the courses offered by the Department in 1963-64 were being taught by men of professorial rank although these courses still did not enroll as many students as those taught by campus clergymen.

The orientation of the Michigan State Department of Religion has been thus far primarily if not overwhelmingly toward teaching. Research has not been a major concern. This is understandable in view of the pressures of enrollment, and of growth, and due to the fact that most of the men who teach the courses have other primary commitments in the form either of pastoral duties or teaching responsibilities in other programs. With the appointment of full-time men in religion, and with an increase in graduate-level teaching, it is very likely that research interest will increase. One professor was a Fulbright Research Scholar at the University of Athens in 1954-56 and another was a Fulbright Research Fellow in India during the 1963-64 academic year. Library resources appear to be adequate to the teaching function for the undergraduate major, and for graduate concentration in certain limited areas.

As it faces the future the Department is confronted with certain necessities and challenges. These include the continuing development of a strong and vital teaching program, the addition of courses in certain religious traditions not now covered or not covered as fully as might be desired (Islam, for example), and the fuller development of graduate work and research. The growth of residence colleges at Michigan State University—where certain basic courses are offered to students in their residence halls—offers a peculiar challenge which the Department probably cannot meet on a wide scale with its limited resources. However, through an influence in such area concentration courses as Humanities in the University College, required of all undergraduates, the Department may be able to exercise an important role in encouraging adequate attention to religious factors in our culture. This type of influence depends largely upon the caliber of the faculty in the Department.

A major question relative to departmental development in the future is that of the availability of funds on a scale not presently realized. While the administrative officers of the University appear to be friendly toward the Department there does not seem to exist any plan for increasing financial support. Like most universities, Michigan State has put its money where need has been greatest in these recent years of rapid expansion. The Department of Religion has managed to keep up with this expansion and with increased enrollments surprisingly well, but it has done so on very limited funds. Efforts have been made to secure outside help on a major scale, but thus far to no avail. It is obvious that if the Department is to capitalize on its present potential it will need substantially more support in the next decade than it has had up to now. Such support is needed primarily for the addition of full-time teachers and scholars of established reputation or of demonstrated potential. For in the final analysis it is first-rate men who create programs of excellence.

Michigan State University: Department of Religion; Faculty—1963-64

HARRY H. KIMBER, *Professor and Chairman of Department*
Degrees: University of Michigan, A.B. 1925; M.A. 1928; Ph.D. 1932.
Author: Kimber and Nulle, eds., *Readings in the History of Civilization,* 2 vols. (1947, 1948). Contributor, McGrath, *Humanities in General Education,* 1949. Contributor, Setton and Winckler, *Great Problems in European Civilization,* 1964. McLean and Kimber, *Teaching of Religion in State Universities,* University of Michigan, Office of Religious Affairs, 1960. Articles, *Journal of Higher Education, Religious Education.* Various other articles and reviews.

ROBERT T. ANDERSON, *Associate Professor*
Degrees: Syracuse University, A.B. 1950; Boston University, School of Theology, S.T.B. 1953; Boston University, Ph.D. 1957.
Dissertation: "Attitude of the Pre-Exilic Canonical Prophets Toward the Cultus."
Author: Various scholarly articles.
Fulbright Research Fellow: India, 1963-64.

FRANCIS M. DONAHUE, *Associate Professor*
Degrees: Michigan State University, M.A. 1948; St. Francis Seminary, S.T.D. 1950; Michigan State University, Ph.D. 1953.
Dissertation: "The Role of Platonism in Greek Orthodox Slavophilism."

Author: With Humphrey, "Changing Bureaucracy and Social Power in a Chicago Ukrainian Parish," *Human Organization,* Summer, 1952; various scholarly articles.

Fulbright Research Scholar: University of Athens, Greece, 1954-56.

PETER B. FISCHER, *Associate Professor*

Degrees: Classical Gymnasium, Czechoslovakia, A.B. 1934; Charles University, Prague, B.D. 1938; University of Chicago, Ph.D. 1942.

Dissertation: "Concept of Sin in Luther's Theology."

Author: "What's in a Classic? The Unity of Augustine's *Confessions*," *Centennial Review,* vol. II, No. 1, Winter, 1958.

W. FRED GRAHAM, *Instructor*

Degrees: Tarkio College, Missouri, A.B. 1952; Pittsburgh Theological Seminary, B.D. 1955; Louisville Presbyterian Seminary, Th.M. 1958; Candidate Ph.D., State University of Iowa.

Dissertation in progress: "The Social and Economic Thought of John Calvin in Theory and Practice in Geneva."

SHAO CHANG LEE, *Professor Emeritus*

Degrees: Yale, A.B. 1917; Columbia, A.M. 1918.

Author: China: Ancient and Modern, 1937, 1940. *Popular Buddhism in China,* 1939. "Chinese Literature," *Encyclopedia of Literature,* Joseph T. Shipley, ed., 1946. "Chinese Literature," *The World Through Literature,* Charlton Laird, ed. *Chinese Houses and Gardens,* ed.; author, chap. V, 1940, 1950, 1963. *"China's Cultural Development"* (A large chart), 1952, 1956.

Lecturers:

THE REV. THEODORE K. BUNDENTHAL
Concordia Seminary, B.A. 1952, B.D. 1954; Washington University, M.A. 1958; Candidate Ph.D., University of Chicago.
Martin Luther Chapel (Missouri Synod).

THE REV. JOHN S. DULEY
Ohio State University, B.S. 1943; Union Theological Seminary, B.D. 1949.
United Campus Christian Fellowship.

RABBI PHILIP FRANKEL
University of Cincinnati, A.B. 1932; Hebrew Union College, B.H. 1931, M.H.L. 1935, D.D. (honorary) 1961.
Shaarey Zedek Congregation.

The Rev. Robert Gardner
Tufts University (Mass.), A.B. 1952; Episcopal Theological School, S.T. B. 1952.
All Saints Episcopal Church.

The Rev. John G. Harrison
University of Texas, B.A. 1950; Austin Presbyterian Theological Seminary, B.D. 1952, Th.M. 1959.
Christian Faith and Higher Education Study Center

The Rev. Robert E. Kavanaugh
Sacred Heart Seminary, A.B. 1957; Catholic University, Washington, D.C., M.A. 1955.
St. John's Catholic Student Center.
Article, "Problems at State University," *America,* April 20, 1963, p. 540.

The Rt. Rev. Msgr. Jerome V. MacEachin
Sacred Heart Seminary, A.B. 1928; Catholic University, Washington, D.C., M.Ed. 1938.
St. Thomas Aquinas Church.

The Rev. Walter R. Wietzke
Capital University, Ohio, B.A. 1943; Evangelical Lutheran Seminary, B.D. 1948; Chicago Lutheran Graduate School, M.S.T. 1954.
University Lutheran Church.

Rabbi Abraham Zemach
University of Minnesota, B.S. 1936; Jewish Theological Seminary of America, M.H.L. 1941.
Hillel Foundation of B'nai B'rith.

---

1. From the dittoed catalogue statement of the Department of Religion, 1964-65 issue.

2. Course descriptions taken from dittoed catalogue statement of the Department of Religion, 1964-65 issue, and from course outlines.

III

A DEPARTMENT OF PHILOSOPHY AND RELIGION:

Western Michigan University, Kalamazoo

Expansion, excitement and enthusiasm—nothing less will do in describing the atmosphere on the campus of Western Michigan University. This institution, which became a university by virtue of legislative act in 1957, has seen its enrollment almost double in the last five years. It is now the fourth largest institution of higher education in Michigan. Through all of this it has managed to maintain or develop an educational program of quality in various areas and to establish one of the more interesting and exciting curricular programs in religion among tax-supported institutions in the United States.

Western Michigan University is of special interest to this study because of its status as an "emerging" state university and because it has managed to develop an impressively successful curricular program in religion in a surprisingly short period of time—less than a decade. In structure and rationale this program also differs considerably from the programs in the two sister Michigan universities already described.

History, Rationale, and Present Status

Western Michigan University was founded as Western State Normal School in 1903. It became Western Michigan College of Education in 1941. Even up to the present time 43 per cent of its graduates possess the certificate to teach at the elementary or secondary level. However, Western is known for its work in a wide variety of areas in addition to teacher education—including such diverse areas as paper technology, occupational therapy, orientation and mobility of the blind, and the recently established Institute of Regional Studies, which seeks—with the help of a liberal grant from the Carnegie Corporation—to improve the training of faculty in non-Western areas and to foster the development of interdepartmental minors in area studies of the non-Western World. Degrees granted by Western include Bachelor of Arts, Bachelor of Business Administration, Bachelor of Music, Bachelor of Science, Bachelor of Science in Engineering, Master of Arts, Master of Business Administration, and Specialist in Education. The institution is largely regional, with over 50 per cent of its students coming from Southwest Michigan and more than 90 per cent from that state.

In 1953 Western was chosen as one of fifteen teacher education institutions to become a pilot center for the Danforth Foundation-financed project on teacher education and religion carried out under the direction of the American Association of Colleges for Teacher Education. A local committee made up of faculty members and administrators was given the task of studying the relevance of religion in the curricular offerings at Western. The major recommendation of this committee was that a department of philosophy and religion be established. The chairman of that committee, Mr. Leonard Gernant, who was Dean of the Chapel at that time, has described developments subsequent to the committee's recommendation:

> Two courses were approved and published in the catalogue, to be taught as soon as an instructor could become available. The courses were called "Introduction to Religion" and "The World of the Old Testament." The original intent of the committee was to use the well-established practice of many other state-owned institutions that employ local clergy who are academically qualified to teach such courses on campus. Since it was not possible to secure complete support for this point of view, the committee turned its efforts toward adding a regular faculty member who would teach courses in religion as part of his assignment. This aim was achieved with the addition to the faculty of Dr. Cornelius Loew as Associate Professor of Religion and Philosophy . . . .[1]

The appointment of Cornelius Loew to the faculty of Western Michigan in 1956 was assisted by a grant from the Danforth Foundation, made in connection with the Foundation's special program for helping in the creation of departments of religion. The grant provided for one-half of Dr. Loew's salary for three years; the other half was paid by Western Michigan. At the end of the three-year period the University assumed full responsibility for the department.

Both the time and the man were right. The story of what has happened since 1956 may be told in various ways. Enrollment in courses in religion has climbed from 115 during the first year of Professor Loew's appointment to approximately 1,000 in the 1963-64 academic year. In the same time period the number of faculty has been increased from one man—who also devoted part of his time to teaching courses in philosophy—to four men who teach full time in the area of religion (and three full time in philosophy. Philosophy and religion are now regarded as separate fields of study, joined in one department for administrative reasons. This description is concerned only with developments in the area of religion.) The Director of the Honors Program at Western Michigan has described the curricular program in religion as one of the most exciting in the University. This he attributed to course content and to the quality of the teaching. Students from a wide variety of areas of specialization and of a consistently high caliber elect courses in religion. (Three of Western Michigan's five nominees for Danforth Graduate Fellowships for 1964-65 were religion majors. The other two had also taken courses in this area. The nominee for a Rhodes scholarship was also a religion major.) The Department has consistently attempted to provide a high quality program with courses of substance. Its grading policies are well in line with the University level, actually being more rigorous than the average.

One of the more interesting and significant aspects of the program at Western Michigan is the conscious effort to provide for the study of major religious traditions—usually, although not always, "from within." This was most dramatically evidenced in the appointment of Jesuit theologian John A. Hardon to the faculty as an Associate Professor on salary from the University in the Fall of 1962. This appointment attracted considerable attention because Dr. Hardon was the first teacher of the Roman Catholic faith to join the Department of Philosophy and Religion and the first ordained priest to be paid out of state funds as a regular member of a department of religion in a state university in the United States. However, seen in the perspective of departmental history and planning, this appointment was a quite natural and logical development. That is, the Department has sought from its beginning to approach the subject of religion theologically as well as philosophically and historically, and to include the beliefs and practices of major religious traditions among its chief concerns and areas of inquiry. Professor Loew himself is a Protestant theologian and all appointments have involved men who have had some theological training. Areas of specialization represented in the faculty in 1963-64 were Protestant theology, Roman Catholic theology, historical theology (especially seventeenth century Protestant "scholasticism"), religion and literature, and philosophy of religion. The next logical step is the appointment of a scholar in Judaism—a step which will be attempted in the near future. The Department has appointed a scholar in the history of religions for the academic year 1964-65. He teaches in the areas of the religions of pre-literates and the major non-Western religions. This appointment fits quite logically not only into the structure and orientation of the Department but also into the work of the Institute of Regional Studies.

By approaching the subject of religion theologically as well as philosophically and historically the Department has endeavored to get at the meaning and significance of religious life and experience as seen by the religious communities themselves and by articulate men of faith. The approach is still basically descriptive (not normative), but descriptive in such a fashion as to enable the students to come to grips with the meaning and significance of religious faith and life both historically and contemporaneously, both for peoples and communities of the past and for their own lives in the world today. This is done not only by a direct approach to theology as such (Fundamentals of Catholic Theology and Twentieth Century Protestant Theologians, for example), but also through an analysis of theological implications of various aspects of life and culture—through such courses as Philosophy of Religion, Contemporary Challenges to Christian Thought, and, particularly, The Religious Quest in Modern Literature.

Curriculum

The curricular program in religion at Western Michigan is divided into five areas: history of religions, Biblical studies, history of Christian thought, theology and ethics, and philosophy of religion. The basic course offered in religion is Introduction to Religion in the West, which is described as "a survey of anthropological and historical data which provide a background against which the biblical view of nature, man, and God can be seen and understood; with special emphasis on three modes of religious expression: myth, philosophy, and history."[2] It is a multiple section three-semester hour course geared to the sophomore level, taught by various members of the Department and offered both semesters. Enrollment is limited to forty students per section. The course may be elected by students to fulfill part of the requirement in the Humanities Area in the core curriculum required of all undergraduates. Three major topics are considered in this course: (1) the language of myth and the awareness of depth, in which the content and nature of myths of ancient Egypt, Babylonia and Greece are considered; (2) the language of philosophy and the awareness of structure, in which emphasis is laid upon ancient Greek philosophy—especially Plato and Aristotle; and (3) the language of revelation and the awareness of the drama of history, in which the major stress is on the development of the faith of ancient Israel—especially as expressed in the Old Testament. The reading requirements in 1963-64 included: Malinowski, *Magic, Science and Religion;* Frankfort, *Before Philosophy;* Guthrie, *The Greeks and Their Gods* and *The Greek*

Philosophers; and Wright, *The Old Testament Against Its Environment.*

Two other courses are offered at the sophomore level: Foundations of Christian Thought, which is described as an "examination of the role of myth, philosophy, and history as modes of religious expression in the development of Christian thought during the first five centuries," and which is a three-semester hour course offered both semesters; and Fundamentals of Catholic Theology, a "study of the principal doctrines of Roman Catholicism, seen in their historical context and examined within the framework of contemporary religious culture"—also a three-semester hour course offered both semesters.

Courses offered at the junior-senior level include: Hinduism and Buddhism; The Shaping of Religion in America—"the histories of Judaism, Protestantism, and Roman Catholicism in the United States, including a survey of distinctive beliefs and practices characteristic of these three traditions at the present time"; Understanding the Old Testament; Understanding the New Testament; Representative Christian Thinkers I—late Middle Ages and early Reformation period; Representative Christian Thinkers II—Protestant theologians of the Reformation and post-Reformation period; Twentieth Century Protestant Theologians; Catholic Moral Theology; Introduction to the Philosophy of Religion; Contemporary Challenges to Christian Thought—"intellectual challenges to Christian thought in the works of Darwin, Feuerbach, Marx, Nietzsche, and Freud"; Twentieth Century Philosophers of Religion; and The Religious Quest in Modern Literature. All of these are three-semester hour courses. Catholic Moral Theology is offered both semesters. The Department also offers independent study at the senior level. No prerequisites other than class level are required for the taking of any course. Enrollments in these courses in recent years are listed in Table III.

A major in religion requires a minimum of 24 semester hours and must include the following courses: Introduction to Religion in the West, Foundations of Christian Thought, Hinduism and Buddhism, either Understanding the Old Testament or Understanding the New Testament, at least one additional course in the area of theology and ethics and one additional course in the area of philosophy of religion. Cognate courses are recommended in philosophy, history, Latin, and Greek. A minor in religion requires a minimum of 15 hours, including Introduction to Religion in the West and Foundations of Christian Thought.

TABLE III

Enrollments in Courses in Religion: Western Michigan University*

Course	'56-'57		'57-'58		'58-'59		'59-'60		'60-'61		'61-'62		'62-'63		'63-'64	
	I	II	I	II	I	II	I	II	I	II	I	II	I	II	I	II
Intro. Religion	26	67	46	42	36	81	47	80	80	86	130	130	185	160	177	145
Fundamentals of Catholic Theology													70	104	110	100
Catholic Moral Theology														51	60	85
Old Testament	6		8				29		30		36		16		16	
New Testament		19		15		25		30		29		30		23		45
Intro. Philosophy of Religion				18		15		18		20	21	16	16			
Contemp. Challenges to Christian Thought																17
20th Century Philosophy of Religion					13		14								17	
Religious Quests in Modern Literature									8	8	7				17	25
Representative Christian Thinkers I																
Representative Christian Thinkers II														10		8
Shaping of Religion in America					14		17	21		25	25	35	20	34		45
Hinduism and Buddhism				6		29						15			(3)†	35
Foundations of Christian Thought																30
20th Century Protestant Theologians									2	2	2	3	2	4	10	10
Independent Studies						2	3	3	2	2	2	3	2	4	6	8
Totals by Semester	32	86	54	81	63	152	117	145	137	178	200	260	309	405	453	528
" Year	118		135		215		262		315		460		714		981	

*Enrollment figures supplied by the Department of Philosophy and Religion.

†*Special Study.*

Summer enrollments: Shaping of Religion (1959) 24; Introduction to Religion (1962) 31, (1963) 32.

While most students who take courses in religion are not majoring in the subject, there were approximately 15 undergraduate majors and 25 minors in 1963-64. Some graduate level work was also available, but the Department is at present resisting any push toward graduate work. The Department conceives of itself as functioning primarily and fundamentally in terms of the liberal education aims of the School of Liberal Arts and Sciences.

One of the more immediate practical concerns of the Department has to do with the core requirement for all undergraduates. Ever since the Department was organized certain courses in religion have been "temporarily" permitted as substitutes for part of the core requirement in the Humanities Area. (As many as 30 per cent of the students who took Introduction to Religion in the West in 1962-63 indicated that they had done so to fulfill this requirement.) Should this "temporary" permission be withdrawn by faculty action the Department could well anticipate a drop in enrollment. However, appointments to the religion faculty have been of such a caliber thus far to attract a considerable number of students on a purely elective basis. Furthermore, the Department has been able to relate itself significantly to both the general studies and the Honors programs at Western Michigan—thus fitting into the liberal arts context and not becoming an isolated academic unit concerned solely with a segmented area labeled "religion."

One section of Introduction to Religion in the West has been offered as a part of the special program for Honors students in General Studies. A new course, Religion and Culture, is being planned as a second contribution of the Department to the Honors College program. Three members of the Department have also participated in the teaching of the regularly required general studies course in the Humanities Area.

Conclusions

The history of the Department of Philosophy and Religion affords an interesting and instructive example of what can be done in the development of the study of religion in an "emerging" state university when vigorous and imaginative leadership is exercised. There is little doubt in this observer's mind that the success of this Department has been due primarily to the central role played in its development by Professor Loew. At the same time, it is evident that he has been significantly helped in his work by the interest and support of some members of the University faculty and of a concerned administration.

Other aspects of the Department's development which, in this observer's opinion, have contributed to its substantial success include: (1) the development of a curricular structure which is concerned with the direct study of religion and primarily, although not exclusively, with the major religious heritage of the West—its origins, development, present manifestations, and its relationships to Western culture; (2) the appointment of a faculty educated primarily in and concerned with the study of various aspects of religion—and especially the religious traditions of the West—and selected with an eye to teaching ability as well as scholarly potential or achievement; (3) the rather constant effort that has been made to establish and maintain standards of excellence in the courses offered; and (4) the early distinction made within the Department—both in terms of curricular structure and faculty—between the areas of philosophy and religion, areas which obviously overlap but which today tend to be quite different in subject matter and approach.

Some questions arise when one considers the continuing development of the Department. Much will depend upon the selection of an able replacement for Professor Loew—who has taken a full-time administrative position at Western Michigan. While one is impressed with the quality of teaching in the field of religion, it is also evident that the teaching load of an average of twelve semester hours could become a problem since it does limit the amount of time available to faculty members for independent study and research. The Department has been able to attract able younger men for its faculty. (The average age of the staff is under forty.) One wonders what might happen as these younger men become more mature and develop their scholarly interest in a more intensive fashion and as possible pressures of additional enrollment (Western Michigan anticipates a "ceiling" of 20,000 students in 1970) increase. Also involved is the subject of the further possibility of concentrated work in religion which would enable faculty members to work intensively with undergraduate and graduate majors. Can the Department of Philosophy and Religion at Western Michigan continue to maintain its liberal arts emphasis and its outreach to students from a variety of areas while also encouraging the development of not only an able teaching faculty but able research scholars as well? Whatever the answers to these questions may be, the fact remains that the Department as presently constituted, and considering its brief history, is interesting in rationale, substantial in quality of courses and teaching, and sound in financial support. All-in-all this augurs well for the future.

Selected Biographical Information: Religion Faculty,
Western Michigan University—1963-64

OTTO GRUNDLER, *Assistant Professor*

Arbitur, Gymnasium Nordhorn, Germany, 1939-47; Western Theological Seminary, B.D. 1950; University of Göttingen, 1950-52; Princeton Theological Seminary, Th.D. 1961; doctoral dissertation, "Thomism and Calvinism in the Theology of Girolamo Zanchi (1516-90)."

Article: "The Influence of Thomas Aquinas upon the Theology of Girolamo Zanchi," *Studies in Medieval Culture.*

JOHN A. HARDON, S.J., *Associate Professor*

John Carroll University, A.B. 1936; Loyola University, Chicago, M.A. 1941; Dogmatic Theology, Gregorian University in Rome, S.T.D. 1951.

Publications: Approximately seventy full-length articles in various journals in the United States and Europe, including *La Civilta Cattolica* (Rome), *Ecclesia* (Madrid), and *Theological Studies; Protestant Churches of America* (1956), translated as *Las Eglesias Protestantes de America* (Mexico City, 1959) ; *All My Liberty* (1959) ; *Christianity in Conflict* (1959) ; *For Jesuits* (1963) ; *Religions of the World* (1963) ; Co-author with Thomas Diehl, *Teaching the Devotion to the Sacred Heart* (1963) ; Contributor and area editor for the "New Catholic Encyclopedia"; consultant and contributor for the "Catholic Youth Encyclopedia"; and contributor in the field of theology to "Grolier's" and "Collier's" Encyclopedia and the "Encyclopedia Americana."

MAYNARD L. KAUFMAN, *Instructor*

Bethel College (Kansas), B.A. 1957; University of Chicago Divinity School, M.A. 1963, candidate for Ph.D.

Articles: "Anabaptism as an Existentialist Philosophy of Religion," *Mennonite Life,* July, 1957, January, April, 1958; "Stephen Dedalus and the Gnostic Heresy in Aesthetics," *Quest, A Journal of Opinion,* December, 1962; "Religious Possibilities in the Post-Christian Epoch," *op. cit.,* May, 1963.

E. THOMAS LAWSON, *Assistant Professor*

Northern Baptist College, Chicago, 1951-55; University of Chicago Divinity School, B.D. 1958, M.A. 1961; University of Chicago, Ph.D. 1963.

Doctoral dissertation: "Hartshorne and Tillich: An Essay on the Sovereignty of God."

CORNELIUS LOEW, *Professor and Head*

Elmhurst College, A.B. 1938; Union Theological Seminary, B.D. 1941; Union Theological Seminary, S.T.M. 1942; Columbia University, Ph.D. 1951.

Publications: Modern Rivals to Christian Faith (1956) ; articles.

---

1. "Religion at a State-Owned Institution: The Western Michigan College Story," *Religious Education,* LII, September-October, 1957, p. 381.

2. Course descriptions taken from *Western Michigan University Bulletin: Undergraduate Catalog & Announcements,* 1963-64, pp. 228-230, and from course outlines.

IV

THE STUDY OF RELIGION IN A STATE UNIVERSITY SYSTEM:

The University of California

Background

The University of California is one of the largest and most vigorous universities in the world with a faculty matched in distinction by few other institutions. It is a prime example of what its president has called a "multiversity"—offering systematic study in a vast array of areas, supporting research on numerous frontiers of knowledge, employing over 40,000 people, enrolling nearly 100,000 students (almost 30,000 at the graduate level), listing close to 10,000 courses in its catalogues, and expending approximately half a billion dollars a year on its operations.[1]

While teaching and research in religion do not occupy a conspicuous place in the midst of this size and complexity, nevertheless, in recent years the question has been of sufficient interest to stimulate debate and resolutions among alumni, faculty, and student groups; to command the attention of faculty committees and University administrators; and even to be a topic of discussion in the public press. Thus, a number of significant questions relating to the study of religion have been raised and aired within the University of California complex. For instance, what in fact is being done in the areas of teaching and research in religion? Is it adequate? If not, what more should be done and what should the approach be? Should there be a department of religion? And, perhaps as central as any question, what about the propriety of including religion as a full-scale discipline or field within the context of a tax-supported university? To what extent does the "Wall of Separation" principle play into the decisions that have to be made?

Some of these questions were brought into public focus in the San Francisco area when the Episcopal Bishop of California, the Right Reverend James A. Pike, in a sermon preached at the Cathedral on Thanksgiving Day, 1961, charged that the University of California at Berkeley was not doing justice to the field of religion. Bishop Pike pointed out that such "topflight" universities as Stanford, Yale, Princeton, Harvard, and Columbia maintained departments or special curricula for the systematic study of religion, and then deplored as indefensible the fact that in spite of the rich array of curricular offer-

ings covering "almost all known fields of thought," adequate attention
to religion was lacking at such a great institution of learning as California. In "the whole huge faculty" of this University, he asserted,
there are not included any individuals "selected because of their pro-
found understanding of the Judeo-Christian tradition which is the
principal crankshaft of Western Civilization, or of any of the other
great world religions."

The Bishop's blast brought varied reactions. The Chancellor of the
Berkeley campus of the University, Edward W. Strong, hastened to
point out that "numerous courses on religion" were offered at that
institution and that "many bachelors' degrees" had been granted to
students who had chosen "religion as their major subject." It was
evident that the Bishop "was not aware of all the University activity
in this field." Because there was "some question whether a state-
supported institution should properly have a department of religion,"
the Chancellor pointed out that the University had long taken the
position that "courses in religion should be placed in the various departments and not grouped together in their own." But since many
such courses were already offered on the Berkeley campus, and since
an individual major in religion was available to qualified students,
it appeared to the Chancellor that what was being done was adequate.
If anything further was needed it was "a course in comparative
religion" which he hoped might be added to the curriculum—probably
"in the Philosophy Department."

In a lead editorial supporting the Bishop's argument, the San
Francisco *Examiner* suggested that the Chancellor "is too touchy on
the church-state separation issue. . . . Sectarian indoctrination is not
asked," the editorial pointed out, but only an opportunity for students
to know more about religious history. "It is an absurdity," the editorial concluded, "that a state-supported school, which is supposed to
open the mind to all knowledge, should contribute to closed minds on
one of the basic essentials of a full education."

Shortly thereafter four prominent student leaders on the Berkeley
campus supported the Bishop and the editorial position of the
Examiner. Pointing out that the question of a department of religion
had been an issue at the University of California, Berkeley, for some
time, the students cited the fact that in 1949, "without a dissenting
vote," the Alumni Council had requested that such a department be
established. "The question is very simple," the students concluded:
"How much longer can a great institution like the University of Cali-

fornia continue to exclude from academic inquiry and investigation a great and distinct discipline like religion?"[2]

Some time after this public exchange the President asked the Chief Campus Officers on the five campuses of the University, in consultation with appropriate Academic Senate committees, to review academic offerings in religion, to give their views as to the adequacy of work in "comparative religion," and to recommend whether additional courses should be offered and whether the establishment of a "department of comparative religion" was advisable. Reports from the five campuses indicated that a total of some 112 courses were being offered in the area of religion—including 60 at Berkeley, 5 at Davis, 30 at Los Angeles, 4 at Riverside, and 13 at Santa Barbara. There appeared to be general agreement among the Chief Campus Officers and the appropriate Academic Senate committees that existing offerings were quite adequate to the subject and that departments of comparative religion were neither needed nor desired.[3]

In order to get a first-hand impression of some of these courses in the area of religion and of campus policies, procedures, and trends, the writer studied intensively and at first hand two campuses of the University of California early in 1964. Berkeley was chosen as the oldest and best known of the campuses and as the campus with the most courses listed in the area of religion. The recently formed Graduate Theological Union, made up of Protestant seminaries in the San Francisco Bay area and involving an informal relationship with the Graduate Division of the University of California at Berkeley, also added to interest in the Berkeley Campus.[4] Santa Barbara was chosen as one of the "emerging campuses" of the University and because it was the only one of the five campuses which had a separately listed curricular program in "Religious Studies"—a program which was moving toward departmental status.

---

1. Clark Kerr, *The Uses of the University* (Cambridge, Mass., Harvard University Press, 1963), chap. I, esp. pp. 7-8.

2. Bishop Pike's sermon is summarized in a story in the *Examiner,* November 24, 1961, p. 3. Chancellor Strong's response is described in the San Francisco *Chronicle,* November 25, 1961, p. 15. The *Examiner's* editorial appeared in the November 28, 1961 issue, p. 28. The students' letter was printed in the *Examiner* on December 12, 1961, p. 34. It was signed by the first vice-president of the Associated Students at the University of California, a past senior representative at large to ASUC, and the presidents of the junior and senior classes. The issue also appeared frequently during and after this period in the pages of the *Daily Californian,* student newspaper at Berkeley.

3. Memorandum from the office of the President to the members of the Committee on Educational Policy of the Academic Senate regarding the "Role of the University in Teaching and Research with Reference to Religion," April 12, 1963. This memorandum is reproduced in Appendix I. (The University of California is a highly and carefully organized institution which allows for extensive faculty participation in government. On this subject see Lynn W. Eley, "The University of California at Berkeley: Faculty Participation in the Government of the University," *Bulletin* of the American Association of University Professors, 50, No. 1, March, 1964, pp. 5-13, and *ByLaws and Regulations of the Academic Senate, University of California*, July, 1960 and July, 1963.)

4. The Graduate Theological Union is described in Appendix II.

IV, A
AN "INDIVIDUAL MAJOR" AND VARIOUS RELEVANT COURSES IN RELIGION:
The University of California at Berkeley

A perusal of recent catalogues of the University of California at Berkeley discloses (*a*) the possibility of an "individual major" in religion, such a major to be structured specifically for and by each student desiring it and to be approved by the Dean and the Executive Committee of the College of Letters and Science, and (*b*) a number of courses in or related to religion and offered in various departments. Neither the "individual major" nor the various courses are under the direction of an administrative structure or faculty committee with specific responsibilities in the area of religion. There is neither a department nor an interdepartmental program. What is done in the study of religion is entirely the result of interests of individual faculty members or of the fact that this study falls quite naturally within the purview of certain departments or disciplines.

The "Individual Major" in Religion

For many years a section on "Religion" has been included in the description of individual majors in the College of Letters and Science. Four types of major programs are available to the undergraduate in that College: (1) departmental major programs; (2) group major programs; (3) field major programs; and (4) individual major programs. Forty-five departmental majors are listed in the *Announcement* of the College for 1963-64. Group majors are listed under Communications and Public Policy, Comparative Literature, Genetics, and Social Welfare. Field majors are offered under Biological Sciences, Humanities, Physical Sciences, and Social Sciences. Individual major programs may be structured, according to the *Announcement,* for those "few superior students whose intellectual needs can be met better by an especially designed individual major program. Such a program must be submitted to the Dean for approval by the Executive Committee of the College."

The section on "Religion" in the *Announcement* indicates that

Students interested in the study of religion, either from the standpoint of liberal education, or of preparation for the ministry or some other phase of religious education, may select a major in one of the departments germane to the purpose of the student, or they may propose an individual major.

The following departments are listed as offering appropriate courses for such purposes: Anthropology, Classics, Economics, Education, English, History, Oriental Languages, Philosophy, Psychology, Near Eastern Languages, Sociology, and Social Welfare. Particular attention is directed to specific courses under History, Near Eastern Languages, and Philosophy.[1]

College records indicate that the number of students choosing the individual major in religion has been very small: 1956, 1957, 1958, one each; 1959, four; 1960, figures not available; 1961, one; 1962, 1963, none. One of the recommendations of the faculty Committee on Courses, in its report to the President on teaching and research in religion at Berkeley (referred to above) is that the faculty consider the possibility of a group major in religion. Such a major would be interdepartmental, would be more obviously structured than an individual major, and would be supervised by a committee with certain individuals designated as advisors. As of the Spring of 1964 no steps had been taken to implement this recommendation.

Courses in or Related to Religion

The question of how many courses are offered in religion at Berkeley depends, quite naturally, on one's understanding of what constitutes such a course. The faculty Committee on Courses reported to the President that sixty courses were being offered in this area, six of which "are concerned entirely with aspects of religion." The Committee did not identify these courses. On the narrowest construction, one might conclude, with the Committee, that only six courses deal *entirely* with aspects of the subject. A broader construction, which also includes courses *related to* the area of religion, could lead to some such figure as sixty or even "over 150"—the latter being a figure attributed to the Chancellor in a story in *The Daily Californian.*[2]

Without intending to enter into a game of numbers, I shall deal cursorily with catalogue course descriptions and then proceed to a more detailed description of some of the offerings which appear to be of greatest interest and significance in terms of the systematic study of religion.

An examination of the courses listed in the Berkeley *General Catalogue* for 1963-64 discloses eleven courses with the words "religion" or "religious" in the title, including Primitive Religion (Anthropology); Ancient Greek Religion (Classics); Studies in Seventeenth Century Religious Texts (French); Religion and Cult in Ancient Palestine, The Religions of Ancient Iran, and Religion and Cosmology of Ancient Mesopotamia—all in Near Eastern Languages; Philosophy of Religion (Philosophy); Nationalism, Religion, and Ideology: The Search for Authority in the New Nations (Political Science); and Sociology of Religion, offered at both undergraduate and graduate levels, and Religious Doctrines and Social Conduct, in Sociology. Five other courses refer to a specific religious tradition in their titles: Early Christian Art and Seminar in the History of Early Christian and Medieval Art (Art); and Jewish Civilization, Rise and Spread of Islamic Society, and Islamic Institutions (Near Eastern Languages). In addition, there are many other courses that deal with religion in some way, including English Bible as Literature (English); several in History— such as Medieval Institutions and Age of Reformation; several in the History of Art; and such courses as Great Books of East Asia (Oriental Languages) and Great Books of Hebrew Literature (Near Eastern Languages). Enrollments in most of these courses in recent years are listed in Table IV.

While such a listing suggests something of the variety of curricular offerings in or related to religion at Berkeley, a more detailed analysis of some of these affords a fuller impression of the nature and extent of work in this area. Many of the courses offered in the Department of Near Eastern Languages deal directly or indirectly with the religious traditions of the Near East. Relevant lecture courses in the lower division include: Languages and Cultures of the Near East, a full year course (two units each semester) dealing with "the growth, structure, and differentiation of ethnic, religious, and language groups in the Arab states, Israel, Turkey, and Iran;"[3] and Great Books of Hebrew Literature, a two-unit course dealing with Hebrew literature in translation. Relevant upper level courses in Near Eastern Languages include: Ancient Israel, a three-unit course dealing with "the history of Israel from the Patriarchal Age to the end of the Second

TABLE IV

Enrollments in Selected Courses in or Related to Religion: University of California, Berkeley[4]

Course	Year and Semester											
	1956-57		1958-59		1960-61		1961-62		1962-63		1963-64	
	I	II	I	II	I	II	I	II	I	II	I	II
Primitive Religion (Anthrop.)	69		87			143		153		185		160
Ancient Greek Religion (Classics)*												29
English Bible as Literature (English)	131			173	175			193		199		398
Age of Reformation (History)†							43		62			69
Ancient Israel (Near East)‡												21
Great Books of Hebrew Literature (Near East)	16	13	14	16	29	68	51	51		68		61
Jewish Civilization (Near East)												
Religion and Cult in Ancient Palestine (Near East)											20	
Religions of Ancient Iran (Near East)§									24			
Religion and Cosmology of Ancient Mesopotamia (Near East)‖												
Rise and Spread of Islamic Society (Near East)¶			19	16	10		13		12	16	19	26
Islamic Institutions (Near East)‖									18	3		10
Biblical Hebrew Texts (Near East)**									8		12	
Great Books of Eastern Asia (Oriental Languages)	47	88	93	66	113	164	116	190	131	215		
Philosophy of Religion (Philos.)						103		109		42		
Medieval and Early-Modern Thought (Philos.)††										16		
Nationalism, Religion and Ideology; Search for Authority in New Nations (Political Science)‡‡												7
Sociology of Religion (Sociol.)			73			88		60	87		50	
Religious Doctrine and Social Conduct (Sociol.)						50				59		
Sociology of Religion (Sociol.) (Graduate level)								10				13

* Enrollments in earlier years: Fall '55, 12; Fall '57, 14; Fall '59, 20.
† Offered for the first time, Fall '61. ‡ Offered for the first time, Spring '64. § Scheduled first 1963-64; dropped for lack of enrollment.
‖ Offered for the first time, Fall '60. Prior to that, "Religion and Cosmology of Ancient Egypt and Mesopotamia" was offered as a year course.
¶ Offered for first time, 1962-63. Prior to that, "Islamic Civilization" was offered: Fall '60, 9; Fall '61, 13; Spring '62, 11.
** Offered for the first time, Fall '60. Prior to that, "Reading in Hebrew" was offered.
†† Offered for the first time, 1962-63. ‡‡ Offered for the first time, Spring '64. ‡‡ Enrollments in earlier years: Fall '55, 16; Fall '57, 27.

Commonwealth"; Jewish Civilization, three units dealing with "the social, religious, and cultural aspects of Jewish life in the main centers of Asia, Africa and Europe from the time of the coming of Islam to the nineteenth century"; Religion and Cult in Ancient Palestine, a two-unit "study of the cultic institutions of Ancient Israel in the context of its contemporary Palestinian environment"; The Religions of Ancient Iran, a full year course, two units per semester, devoted principally "to the study of Zoroastrianism and Manicheanism"; Religion and Cosmology of Ancient Mesopotamia; and various courses dealing with Islamic society and institutions. An undergraduate student may elect a major emphasizing Assyriology, Egyptology, Hebrew, Arabic, South Asian Languages, Iranology, Semitic Languages, or Islamic Studies. Advanced degree programs are also available in many of these areas.

Often the interests and research of one scholar will stimulate interest in a particular area. This has happened in the Department of Sociology at Berkeley where the work of Dr. Charles Y. Glock, Professor and Director of the Survey Research Center, has brought about considerable interest in the Sociology of Religion. Professor Glock offers two courses in this area, one a three-hour upper division course which presents "a systematic survey including sociological theory and organizational structure of religion, the character of religious authority and leadership, the individual's religion, and the interplay with other spheres of social life"; and the other a two-unit graduate course which examines the "interplay between theory and research," and the "interrelations of religious ideas and institutions with the economic, political, and social order." The most recent available outline for the undergraduate course includes the following main topics:

I. The Scope and Value Premises of the Sociological Study of Religion.

II. A Comparative Overview of the World's Religions.

III. Origin, Development, and Function of Religion.
   A. Evolutionary and Anthropological Views.
   B. Sociological Theory of Religion.
   C. Psychological and Social Psychological Views.

IV. Religious Institutions.
   A. The Nature and Form of Religious Organization.
      1. Early forms of religious organization.
      2. The development of religious organization—church and sect.
      3. The organization of religion in America.
      4. Contemporary church organization and its sociological implications.

B. Religious Authority and Leadership.
  1. Types of religious authority.
    a. Catholic.
    b. Protestant.
    c. Jew.
C. The Individual and His Religion.
  1. Varieties of religious experience.
  2. The social bases of religious commitment.
  3. The social consequences of religious commitment.

V. Institutional Interrelationships.
  A. Religion and the Economic Order.
  B. Religion and the State (Religion and Politics).

Topics discussed in the graduate course in the Sociology of Religion in the Spring semester of 1964 included problems of defining religion, the scope of the sociology of religion, the theology of sociology, religion and social control, religion and social change, the comparative organization of religion, the social sources of denominationalism and ecumenicity, the anatomy of religious commitment, and religion as a profession. Approximately twenty-five graduate students participated in this course. Some graduate students in sociology have chosen Sociology of Religion as one area of concentration, and a few have done or are doing masters' essays or doctoral dissertations in this area. Sociology of Religion is one of Professor Glock's major interests, and as Director of the Survey Research Center of the University of California he has stimulated and engaged in a number of research projects in this field.

Because of his own interest in politics and ideology in the emerging nations, Professor David E. Apter of the Political Science Department has developed a graduate level course with the intriguing title, Nationalism, Religion and Ideology: The Search for Authority in the New Nations. This three-unit seminar deals with "problems of political values, the evolution of legitimate authority, the status of political ideas and religious beliefs, and the search for new political forms in nations which emerged from colonial status after 1945." The text for the seminar is *Old Societies and New States,* Clifford Geertz, ed., and, in some measure, the seminar is organized around the themes discussed in this book. Professor Apter has himself written in the area of concern in the course, including papers on "Ideology and Discontent" and "Political Religion in the New Nations."

"Ancient Greek Religion," taught by Professor Joseph Fontenrose, Chairman of the Classics Department, is an upper division, three-unit course, which consists of an examination of "the worship of the gods in ancient Greece; cults and religious ideas." Topics discussed in the Spring of 1964 included preliminary definitions; forms of Greek worship; gods, godlings, demons; Aegean and early Greek religion; the great festivals; shamanism, oracles, divination; mystery cults; the afterlife; and Greek religious thought. Approximately thirty students enrolled in the course, which has no prerequisite.

The English Bible As Literature has been a standard offering in the English Department for many years. It has recently been offered as a three-unit, upper division course without prerequisite, and has consistently had a relatively large enrollment—ranging from 131 in the Spring of 1957 to approximately 400 in the Spring of 1964. The course was taught in 1964 by Professor John E. Jordan, Vice-Chairman of the English Department, and a specialist in nineteenth century English literature. The text used in the Spring of 1964 was The Reader's Bible (London, 1951). Topics covered in lectures included the history of the Book; the English Bible; prehistory; the patriarchs; the Joseph saga; the Exodus; Moses; the Promised Land; Samuel vs. Saul; King David; Solomon in all his glory; the prophetic voice; Amos; Hosea; I Isaiah; Jeremiah; Ezekiel; II Isaiah; Ruth; Esther and Judith; Jonah and Tobit; Job; Ecclesiastes; Wisdom of Solomon; Proverbs; Hebrew poetry; Psalms; Song of Songs; Daniel; New Testament background; Mark; Matthew; Luke; John; Acts of the Apostles; Paul, apostle to the Gentiles; and The Apocalypse.

Primitive Religion has been a standard and quite popular offering in the Anthropology Department. During the Spring semester of 1964 it was taught by Mr. David B. Eyde, Acting Assistant Professor of Anthropology. The approach to religion in this course was strongly influenced by the French sociological school of Durkheim, Mauss, and Levi-Strauss.

This sampling of courses in or related to religion indicates considerable breadth and some depth which, while it has not entirely satisfied Bishop Pike—and some other critics both off and on the Berkeley campus—did seem quite adequate to the faculty Committee on Courses. The one addition which this Committee recommended in its report to the President was the offering of a course in Comparative Religion. This recommendation was approved by the Chancellor and he has expressed his concern that such a course be included in the offerings in religion at Berkeley. As of the Spring of 1964 it had not been added to the curriculum.

Curricular Structure and Opposition to a Department of Religion

Given the highly organized nature of the modern university, with its departments, institutes, centers, committees, interdepartmental programs, etc.—all designed to achieve and promote systematic study and research in areas of interest and importance to the academic community and to society at large—it might seem surprising to some observers that such a major institution as the University of California at Berkeley has no such specific structure for the encouragement of these ends in the area of religion. But such, in fact, is the case, and the study of religion, as suggested above, is entirely the result of the specific interests of individual faculty members or of the fact that certain departments include this area within their purview. And where the study of religion is included within the curricular structure and subsidized research of a particular department, it is usually not the direct or primary concern of that department, but is a by-product of a primary interest in the study of language, literature, art, philosophy, politics, or the social structure of a particular culture.

There appears to be little disposition within what can be called the academic power structure at Berkeley to recommend or support the establishment of some sort of an administrative and curricular structure which deals directly and primarily with the study of religion. In fact, one is impressed with the strength of the resistance to such a move. The focal point of this resistance, and the point at which it is most vocal, is the question of a department of religion.

Both the faculty Committee on Courses and the Chancellor have taken a formal stand against the establishment of a department of religion at Berkeley. Opposition also appears to have been strong among other faculty members and administrators who have expressed views on this subject. Some suggest that constitutional provisions for separation of church and state prevent a state university in California from establishing a department of religion. The Chancellor raised this question in his response to Bishop Pike's Thanksgiving Day sermon. Another Berkeley administrator pointed out to the author that "our lawyers would not permit" such a department to come into existence. Apparently he had in mind the opinion of a legal advisor who suggested that a department of religion would fall under constitutional prohibition because of the possibility that it would introduce proselyting into the classroom. Some concerned faculty on the Berkeley campus have advanced a more obvious academic reason for opposition to a department of religion: that is that there is no recognizable independent discipline of religion around which to build such a department.[5] These individuals do recognize the history of religions as a legitimate field of scholarly study, but they suggest that its methodological canons place it within the general discipline of history, where it might have the status of a subdiscipline comparable, for example, to the history of science. They also suggest that insofar as theology is a legitimate area of study for a university, it can be handled either as intellectual history or as philosophy of religion or under both rubrics. Some faculty members who have expressed views of this sort have also argued that the present offerings in the area of religion at Berkeley are not sufficient, and have suggested that courses in the history of religions (the history of Christianity, for example) might legitimately be added to the present offerings. But because religion as such, they claim, has not been and is not a recognizable academic discipline, these courses should properly be added within such existing departments as History, Philosophy, and Near Eastern Languages.

Much of the discussion at Berkeley concerning the possibility of a department of religion, and of the whole question of the study of religion, has been carried on in the kind of charged atmosphere which often characterizes such considerations. Some of the ingredients which have contributed perhaps as much heat as light to these discussions include assertions or accusations about the prevailing "secularism" (meaning opposition to religion) on the Berkeley campus and equally vigorous contentions that any direct study of religion is in danger of becoming non- or un-academic (unscientific) because of the doctrinaire, sectarian, self-interested and emotional nature of the practice and practitioners of religion. People who can be called men of good will, both on and off the campus, have entered freely into the discussions.

While high pitched discussions of religion on the campus have probably been taking place off and on since the beginnings of the University, the recent rise in decibel level seems to have been considerably augmented by the Thanksgiving Day, 1961, sermon preached by the Episcopal Bishop of California. Whether the timing was deliberate or not, this sermon was delivered shortly after Edward W. Strong, Professor of Philosophy and one-time Chairman of the Department of Philosophy, had been appointed Chancellor of the Berkeley campus. The effect was to put the new Chancellor on the spot, and, as might have been expected, he reacted sharply and with considerable firmness. Furthermore, anyone familiar with faculty jealousy for academic prerogatives, and with the tradition and degree of faculty participation in government at Berkeley, would have suspected that such opinions expressed by "interested parties" off the campus would arouse considerable resistance among faculty members.

It is perhaps unfortunate that the study of religion cannot be debated on its own merits and according to academic canons and procedures. But, given the nature of religion—which tends to arouse strong opinions—and given the history of the astringencies of church-university relations in this country, calm and "disinterested" discussion of this subject appears to be an entirely unrealistic prospect. In any case, the Berkeley experience offers an interesting and perhaps instructive case study of what can happen when the question of the study of religion becomes a matter of general discussion.

Conclusions

Three questions remain after a review of teaching and research in religion at the University of California at Berkeley: (1) Is the present program, including the possibility of an "individual major" in religion and the various course offerings, adequate to the subject and to the stature and inclusiveness of such a major institution? (2) Is the field of religion of such a nature to warrant either separate departmental treatment or a more obvious formal academic structure than now exists? (3) Are there legal or constitutional provisions which would prevent the University of California at Berkeley from establishing such a structure?

(1) Determination of adequacy is, to a degree, a subjective matter. But one need not necessarily be "religious" to recognize the importance of religion to human life and culture. And if one is willing to grant that religion is one of the major factors in the history and dynamics of human culture, then he can attempt to deal with the question of adequacy on academic grounds and with as little regard as possible for personal interest or involvement. On such grounds, it is evident that while there are quite substantial offerings at Berkeley in some aspects of religion, at the same time other important and relevant aspects of the subject are either touched upon only lightly or not at all. A partial listing of such largely untouched areas would include the history, literature, practices, and beliefs of such major religions as Hinduism, Buddhism, and Christianity, and the relation-

ship between religion and such cultures as those of India, China, Japan, and America.

It is quite obvious that the "individual major" in religion is little more than a catalogue provision. The number of students who have chosen this option is so small as to be insignificant when one considers the size of the undergraduate enrollment at Berkeley. It is true that a determined and resourceful student might be able to secure a fairly substantial amount of academic work in the area of religion, but he would need to devise, largely on his own, a unifying thread in his work and he would be unable to study formally substantial areas of the subject.

The faculty Committee on Courses recommended in its report to the President that the faculty study the possibility of a "group major" in religion—that is one that would be more structured than an "individual major" and would be under the guidance of a faculty committee. The Committee also recommended that a course in "Comparative Religion" be offered at Berkeley. Both of these steps would improve the existing situation—which is one of considerable imbalance and lack of direction in the area of religion. But considering the existing situation, the stature of the University of California at Berkeley, and the nature and importance of religion, these suggested steps appear to this observer to be woefully inadequate. From such an institution one might expect a bold and imaginative program which could contribute substantially to understanding of the nature, function, and history of religion.

(2) The answer to the second question involves both theoretical and practical considerations. The nature of and problems associated with the direct study of religion have been alluded to in the introductory chapter. The question of whether and how scholars engaged in this study will become involved in the academic process of a particular university can, of course, be answered only by that institution. But it is difficult to see any cogent reason why the area of religion should be treated differently from such other aspects of human culture as art and politics, for example. Obviously the study of religion can and does take place in the curricula of history and philosophy departments, as well as elsewhere. It is equally obvious that the study of such areas as art and politics might also be subsumed under these departments. But as traditions of scholarship have grown in art and political science, and as communities of scholars have gained in strength and accomplishment, it has seemed thoroughly appropriate

that separate departments or academic programs — with their own methodologies, systems of concentration, frontier areas of research, budgets, and staffs of scholars—should come into existence and flourish. In the context of the complex modern American university, it is quite apparent that without such a development the study of religion tends to become a largely unstructured affair dependent upon the interests of particular faculty members whose primary competence and concerns lie in other areas. And a collection of courses in various departments is not likely to constitute a coherent and carefully designed curriculum in religion, nor is it likely to give rise to the kind of systematic scholarly pursuit of a particular area which is the hallmark of such a university.

(3) The question of the legality or constitutionality of courses in religion has received considerable attention in the University of California. The most thorough study of the subject supports the conclusion that a curricular structure in religion—such as a department—is within the constitutional provisions of the United States and the State of California so long as the sole purpose of such a structure is the scholarly study of religion.[6] A department of religion has, in fact, been established on one of the campuses and certainly with the permission of the University administration. It is to this development that we now turn.

Biographical and Bibliographical Information on Selected Faculty Members Who Teach Courses Related to Religion; University of California, Berkeley

DAVID E. APTER, *Professor of Political Science and Associate Director, Institute of International Studies*

Antioch, B.A.; Princeton, M.A., Ph.D.

Author: The Gold Coast in Transition, 1959; *Ghana in Transition,* 1963, revised; *The political Kingdom in Uganda: A Study in Bureaucratic Nationalism,* 1961; *A Reader in Comparative Politics,* 1963; and *Ideology and Discontent,* in press; numerous articles and monographs.

WILLIAM M. BRINNER, *Associate Professor of Near Eastern Languages and Acting Chairman of the Department*

University of California, Berkeley, A.B., M.A., Ph.D.
Special field: Islamics.
Author: Articles and monographs.

DAVID B. EYDE, *Acting Assistant Professor of Anthropology*
University of Hawaii, B.A.; Candidate Ph.D. in Anthropology, Yale.

JACOB J. FINKELSTEIN, *Associate Professor of Assyriology and Associate Curator of Mesopotamian Archaeology, Museum of Anthropology, Chairman of the Department of Near Eastern Languages*
Brooklyn College, B.A.; University of Pennsylvania, Ph.D.
Special field: Assyriology
Author: Articles and monographs.

WALTER J. FISCHEL, *Professor of Semitic Languages and Literature*
Studied at Universities of Heidelberg and Frankfurt; University of Giessen, Ph.D.
Special field: Semitics.
Author: Ibn Khaldun in Egypt, Statesman and Historian, 1382-1406, 1964; extensive articles and monographs.

JOSEPH FONTENROSE, *Professor of Classics and Chairman of the Department of Classics*
University of California, Berkeley, A.B., M.A., Ph.D.
Author: Python: A Study of Delphic Myth and Its Origins, 1959; *The Cult and Myth of Pyrros at Delphi,* 1960; *John Steinbeck: An Introduction and Interpretation,* 1963; numerous articles and monographs.

CHARLES Y. GLOCK, *Professor of Sociology, and Director, Survey Research Center*
New York University, B.S.; Boston University, M.B.A.; Columbia University, Ph.D.
Author: Numerous articles and monographs.

WALTER B. HENNING, *Professor of Iranian Studies*
University of Göttingen, Ph.D.
Author: Zoroaster—Politician or Witch-Doctor?, 1951; extensive articles and monographs.

JOHN E. JORDAN, *Professor of English and Vice-Chairman of the Department of English*
University of Richmond, B.A.; Johns Hopkins University, M.A., Ph.D.
Author: Thomas De Quincey: Literary Critic, 1952; *De Quincey to Wordsworth: A Biography of A Relationship,* 1962; articles.

Gene M. Schramm, *Assistant Professor of Semitic Languages*
University of California, Berkeley, A.B., M.A.; Dropsie College,
Ph.D.
Author: Articles.

---

1. *Announcement* of the College of Letters and Science, 1963-64, pp. 35-38.
2. April 24, 1962, p. 1.
3. Course descriptions taken from the *General Catalogue, University of California,*
Berkeley, 1963-64, and from course outlines.
4. Enrollment figures supplied by the Chancellor's office.
5. "The Status of Religion at the University of California, Berkeley," April 25,
1962. A statement signed by nine members of the faculty of the College of Letters
and Science.
6. David W. Louisell, Professor of Law and John H. Jackson, Acting Associate
Professor of Law, University of California School of Law, Berkeley, "Religion,
Theology, and Public Higher Education," *California Law Review,* 50, December,
1962, pp. 751-799.

IV, B

A PROGRAM IN RELIGIOUS STUDIES DEVELOPING INTO A DEPARTMENT:

The University of California at Santa Barbara

The University of California at Santa Barbara is of special significance to this study. Although founded in 1891, and existing since
1909 as a state-supported institution, Santa Barbara became a campus
of the University of California in 1944—as Santa Barbara College—and
was made a general campus of the University only in 1958. Previously
it had been a state college primarily emphasizing teacher education.
As one of the "emerging campuses" of the University of California,
Santa Barbara has experienced rapid growth and development in
recent years, and in a decade or so will probably become one of the
major campuses of the University. Its special significance for this
study, however, lies in the fact that it is the one campus of the University which has developed a formal curricular program in religious
studies, a program which has recently achieved departmental status.
The program is quite modest in its present stage of development, but
it can be expected to grow in importance to Santa Barbara, to the
University generally, and, perhaps to tax-supported institutions elsewhere.

The development of the curricular program in religion at Santa
Barbara is due substantially to the interests and efforts of one faculty

member and to the support he received from some other faculty members and from the University administration. Professor D. Mackenzie Brown, a political scientist with a special interest and competence in Asian and especially Indian political thought, became convinced that students should have an opportunity to study the nature and role of religion in the cultures of East and West and decided to do something about this conviction. In 1958 he was able to institute a special section on "Religious Institutions" within the College of Letters and Science. That same year he announced two courses, one a lecture course on The Western Religious Heritage and the other, a special program of study for individual students under the heading Group Studies in Religious Institutions. These courses were listed in the catalogue under the heading "Religious Institutions" and immediately following the section on Political Science. Two more courses—Contemporary Religious Movements and Comparative Religion—were added to the listing in 1959. A year later "Religious Institutions" became a separate program in the College of Letters and Science and under the direction of a faculty committee composed of Professor Brown, chairman, Professor William F. Kennedy of Economics, and Professor Cornelius H. Muller of Botany. Professor Brown taught most of these courses. He was assisted by a junior staff member in Political Science, and by Professor Kennedy, who taught Contemporary Religious Movements one semester. In 1961 another course—Introduction to Religion—was added to the list.

Significant steps were taken in 1962 with the authorization of a major in "Religious Institutions," the expansion of the faculty committee in charge of the program, and the appointment of Protestant theologian Paul Tillich, as Visiting Professor of Religious Institutions for the second semester of the 1962-63 academic year. In 1963 the title of the program was changed to "Religious Studies" and the first full-time faculty appointment was made in this area. Eight separate courses were offered in 1963-64, and during the same academic year the establishment of a department was approved by faculty and administrative action, Professor Brown was designated chairman-elect, and the Administration authorized the appointment of an additional full-time faculty member to begin work in the Fall of 1964.

Thus within the relatively short period of six years the curricular program in religion at Santa Barbara developed from two offerings, listed as something of an addendum to Political Science offerings, into a separate department with a staff of three full-time men and with the promise of further expansion.

From the beginning, courses in the area of religion have been structured and taught with a primary concern for the nature, history, and role of religion in human culture. Stress has been laid upon the direct study of religion for purposes of increasing knowledge and understanding. The Western religious heritage has received primary attention, but students have also had an opportunity to study the religions of other areas. The rationale, then, which has guided the development of the program in "Religious Studies" has evolved in the context of the academic community itself and it has fitted well into the program and purpose of that community.

Curriculum and Courses

Courses which have been offered in "Religious Studies" include:

Introduction to Religion
> An analytical survey of the historical development and cultural role of religious traditions and institutions.

Religion and Society
> The relationship of religious concepts and values to contemporary problems of individual behavior, political responsibility, and international order.

The Western Religious Heritage
> The Judaic, Greek, and Christian ideas and institutions which constitute the religious traditions of Western civilization.

Contemporary Religious Movements
> The doctrines and practices of religious organizations and movements in the United States.

Comparative Religion
> The origins, development, and doctrines of major world religions.[1]

Various courses of relevance to the study of religion have also been offered in the more established departments, including The English Bible as Literature, in English; several courses in History; Philosophy of Religion and other courses in Philosophy; Primitive Religion in Anthropology; and Asian Thought in the Asian Studies curriculum.

The major in "Religious Studies" has been developed in such a fashion as to fit into the broad spectrum of humanistic learning. It is described as being "designed for students desiring a general education with emphasis upon" the religious "aspect of Western civilization and comparative cultures." In preparation for the major, students must take full-year courses in the History of Europe and the History of

Philosophy, and the two lower division courses in "Religious Studies," i.e., Introduction to Religion and Religion and Society. The major itself requires "twenty-four units of upper division Religious Studies courses," including Comparative Religion. Six of the twenty-four units may be selected from Primitive Religion (offered in Anthropology), Philosophy of Religion, or other related courses.[2] Thus the major is one which draws upon relevant courses in other departments while requiring a solid core of work in "Religious Studies" itself.

During the 1963-64 academic year three men taught eight separate courses—a total of thirty semester hours—in the program in "Religious Studies." Courses offered in addition to the five already listed and described above included Contemporary Trends in Religious Thought, Religion and the Humanities, and the course for individual students called Group Studies in Religious Institutions. The total enrollment for the year was approximately 200, and there were two majors in "Religious Studies."

The Developing Department

It appeared in the Spring of 1964 that prospects for the soon-to-be-established Department of Religious Studies were quite bright. Plans for the transition from program into department included the continued functioning, for the immediate future, of the faculty Committee-in-Charge of the present program in "Religious Studies." In effect, one gathered, this Committee which is made up of professors and associate professors from other departments will act in lieu of a senior staff until the Department is well established. The departmental staff was to be augmented by the appointment of an additional full-time faculty member, at the junior level, in the Fall of 1964 and by the return of Dr. Paul Tillich as Visiting Professor during part of the 1964-65 academic year. Prospective departmental fortunes were further improved with the announcement in the Summer of 1964 of a grant from the Danforth Foundation which will underwrite one-half the salary of the Chairman during the first three years of the Department's existence.

Plans for the future involve a continuing effort to broaden and deepen curricular offerings, to relate these offerings to the educational program of the College of Letters and Science, and to enhance the opportunities for specialization in religious studies. Requirements for degrees in the College of Letters and Science include a certain amount of course work under the heading of "General Education." None of the courses in "Religious Studies" has been included among the options listed in this area. It is anticipated that two to four of these

TABLE V

Enrollments in Selected Courses in Religious Studies:
*University of California, Santa Barbara**

Course	1958-59		1959-60		1960-61		1961-62		1962-63		1963-64	
	I	II	I	II	I	II	I	II	I	II	I	II
Intro. Religion 30										43	38	29
Religion and Society 40											13	35
Western Religious Heritage 101A-101B	15			15	13		24		16		7	5
Contemporary Religious Movement 102			5					19			4	
Contemporary Trends in Religious Thought 103												10
Biblical Judaism and Christianity 110†												
Comparative Religion 151		27				18						40
Indian Religions 160†												
Religion and Humanities 170											4	
Christianity and Encounter of World Religions 180										18		
Group Studies in Religious Institutions 194A-194B								2	2	7		
Totals in Religious Studies	15	27	5	15	13	18	24	21	18	68	66	119

Enrollments in Courses in Related Areas

Course	1958-59		1959-60		1960-61		1961-62		1962-63		1963-64	
	I	II	I	II	I	II	I	II	I	II	I	II
English 116. English Bible as Literature	22	31	32	33	34	30	38	38	58	66	69	
Asian Studies 187. Asian Thought	21		26			2		1				
Philosophy 112. Philosophy of Religion	34						32				28	
Anthropology 124. Primitive Religion	24					37	37	54	32	67	66	
Majors in Religious Studies (Approved Fall 1963)											2	2

* Enrollment figures supplied by the Department of Religious Studies, and the office of the Registrar.

† Listed in the catalogue but not offered as of 1963-64.

courses will be recommended to the faculty for inclusion as appropriate options. If this action is successful it could have the effect of increasing enrollments in the courses granted this status. It is also expected that the major in "Religious Studies" will become attractive to more students as the faculty is expanded and the number of courses increased. The question of specialization at the graduate level has not been seriously considered, but will no doubt be a matter for discussion as the Department develops.

Plans for augmenting faculty in the Department included the appointment of scholars in church history in the Fall of 1964, and in Biblical studies and religion and society, at later dates. One of the faculty members of professorial rank in the program in 1963-64 specialized in the area of non-Western, and especially Indian religious development, and the other was trained as a philosophical theologian, with a special interest in recent religious thought in the West.

The long range future of the Department will depend very much on its ability to attract producing scholars to its faculty and students to its courses. It is of interest to note that the University has a working agreement with its source of support which calls for the employment of additional faculty members on the basis of increase in enrollment. Thus as the student load increases by a certain amount in a particular department, that department may be authorized to add to its faculty. As of 1963-64 the courses in "Religious Studies" had not enrolled a sufficient number of students to warrant the appointment of an additional full-time faculty member under the agreed-upon formula. However, since "Religious Studies" is a developing area, it can be and is argued that this area should be "subsidized" for the immediate future. But the logic of the system would seem to indicate that the Department will need more and more to carry its own weight, that is, to enroll an increasing number of students. Considering the skill and insight with which the program in "Religious Studies" has been developed in its short history, and given the fact of rapidly expanding enrollments at Santa Barbara, it does not take much of a stretch of the imagination to conclude that this may quite easily be accomplished within the span of another six years.

Conclusions

If the curricular programs in religion in the three Michigan institutions described above reveal contrasts within one state, the programs in the two University of California campuses considered here offer a striking example of dissimilarities within one state university system.

Two facts stand out in particular: (1) Berkeley, the older, more established and more highly developed institution, offers a richer curricular program in such areas as Near Eastern studies and the sociology of religion while Santa Barbara has developed a more obvious and more coherent curriculum in "Religious Studies" as such. (2) One is also impressed with the fact that, while a Department of Religious Studies has been established on one campus, such a development has been strongly opposed on the other.

What are the factors which account for the rather remarkable developments at Santa Barbara—and, in particular, for the establishment of a department? No doubt the fact that Santa Barbara is one of the newer campuses in the University system and that it is in a state of flux and rapid growth has contributed to a relatively greater openness to new developments in this area than one finds on a more well established campus such as Berkeley. The support of the University administration was decisive to the development of the program. In fact, there would have been no Department of Religious Studies without the approval and support of President Clark Kerr and Chancellor Vernon I. Cheadle in particular. Professor Brown's approach and work was obviously of considerable importance to the whole development. His own interest in the political thought of Asia, and especially India, and his research and travels in connection with this interest, led him quite naturally to an interest in the role of religion in human culture. Just as a systematic study of Hinduism is necessary to an understanding of the institutions and ideologies of India, so a fuller acquaintance with the Western religious heritage can contribute to a profounder grasp of Western social and political ideas and practices. To what extent this particular line of reasoning may have provided the background for Professor Brown's own developing concern that students might be given an opportunity systematically to study religious institutions and thought is beside the point. He did, however, manage to put his concern for the study of religion into practice and to do so in a persuasive and well conceived fashion. And in the process he secured the support of some key faculty members who shared his concern. One of these was an economic theorist, a Roman Catholic in personal religious affiliation, who was persuaded not only to serve on the faculty committee in charge of the program in "Religious Institutions" (later "Religious Studies"), but who also taught a course on Contemporary Religious Movements. Another was a distinguished botanist, a man with no formal religious affiliation, but one who shared Professor Brown's conviction that students should have an opportunity to study religion under proper academic conditions. Other members of the faculty committee have included two different members of the Philosophy Department and a professor of music. Thus support for the development of the program in "Religious Studies" has come from a variety of faculty members representing much of the academic spectrum at Santa Barbara. This support has been won primarily on academic or scholarly grounds—not out of any special sort of pious pleading or as a result of pressure from "religious" individuals or groups on or off the campus. Significantly, then, the case has been made on the premises that the study of religion is a valid and important academic endeavor in the university dedicated as it is to the pursuit of knowledge.

No doubt Professor Paul Tillich's brief participation in the program in "Religious Studies" contributed substantially to its continuing development as a program of substance in an academic context. While the enrollment in his course on Christianity and the Encounter of World Religions was limited to eighteen, his influence was felt beyond those particular students. His scholarly approach and his broad understanding of the nature of religion and the relationship between religion and culture made a significant impact on the whole campus community. Indeed, the presence of a man of his stature on the University faculty may have had a significant effect in bringing about the favorable faculty and administrative action on the question of establishing a Department of Religious Studies.

While the development of the curricular program in "Religious Studies" has had a considerable amount of faculty support, there has also been some resistance to it. Some have objected on quite legitimate academic grounds—raising the question of the nature of religion as an academic discipline or field, for example. The question of legality has also been raised by a few; and some have implied that a curricular program in religion should be resisted because of the dangers of introducing piety or proselyting, or the "bootlegging of God," into the curriculum. The development has probably also encountered the normal amount of resistance springing from individual and departmental jealousies over students. Whatever the nature and extent of faculty objection and resistance to it, however, the fact is that a department has been authorized by the proper faculty committees and administrative authorities. To one familiar with the degree of faculty control over curriculum in the University of California system, this speaks volumes about the academic tenability of the curricular program in "Religious Studies." Furthermore, it appears that the Department can gain further faculty (and student) support as it effectively goes about its legitimate business of systematically engaging in the scholarly study of religion. The decisive factor, of course, will be the continuing appointment of competent scholars who can gain the respect of their colleagues and peers for an area of study which to a greater degree than many others has had to prove its case for recognition.

Faculty Teaching in the Department of Religious Studies;
University of California, Santa Barbara—1964-65

DONALD MACKENZIE BROWN, *Professor of Political Science, Chairman of the East Asian Studies Program, and Chairman of the Department of Religious Studies*

B. 1908; Political Science, Stanford, Ph.D.

Author: The White Umbrella, Indian Political Thought from Manu to Gandhi; China Trade Days, Selected Letters from the Thompson Papers; and The Nationalist Movement, Indian Political Thought from Ranade to Bhave.

WALTER H. CAPPS, *Lecturer*

Portland State College, B.S.; Augustana Theological Seminary, B.D.; Yale University Divinity School, S.T.M.; Yale University, M.A., Candidate Ph.D. (historical theology).

WILLIAM RICHARD COMSTOCK, *Assistant Professor*

B. 1928; University of California, Berkeley, B.A.; Princeton Theological Seminary, B.D., Th.M.; Union Theological Seminary, Th.D. (philosophical theology).

Author: "Further Fascination of the Ontological Argument," *Union Seminary Quarterly Review, XVIII,* March 1963, pp. 250-255; various reviews in *Union Seminary Quarterly Review.*

PAUL TILLICH, Ph.D., *Visiting Professor*

---

1. Course descriptions taken from the *General Catalogue, University of California, Santa Barbara,* 1963-64, p. 203.
    2. *Ibid.*

V

A DEPARTMENT OF RELIGION:

The University of North Carolina

History, Rationale, and Curriculum

The University of North Carolina is the oldest American state
university. Its Department of Religion, however, is of quite recent
origin, although some kind of study of religion has been offered
almost continuously since 1795, when the University first admitted
students. From the very beginning, for instance, North Carolina's
curriculum has included courses in Bible and Biblical literature.
Then, early in the 1920's, chiefly on the initiative of certain church
representatives, attempts were made to institute credit courses in
Bible taught in "Bible chairs" by denominational representatives—
similar to the pattern at the University of Texas. These efforts were
denied by the University administration on both legal and educational
grounds. Later, in 1926, an independent Chapel Hill School of
Religion was founded by denominational leaders and interested University personnel. Non-credit courses were offered by this School for
two years, but the whole concept was abandoned when in 1928 the
faculty of the University denied a petition that these courses be
granted university credit and adopted a University resolution recommending to the Trustees

> the inclusion in the University curriculum of instruction in the
> history and literature of religions on the same basis as instruction
> is given in other fields of human activity to be given by instructors
> to be chosen by the Board of Trustees of the University.

The Trustees later adopted a similar resolution. Relevant existing
courses were singled out for continuation (such as New Testament
Greek, and Ethics) while other courses were subsequently introduced
for the first time (such as Old Testament History, The Archaeology of
the Bible, Comparative Literature of the Bible, Comparative Religions.) Most of these courses were offered throughout the 1930's and
1940's and two or three of them have continued down to the present
time.[1]

Thus the faculty and trustee actions of 1928 clearly stated the policy
that the University itself should assume full responsibility for instruction in the areas of Bible and religion and that this instruction
should be carried out on the same basis and in the same manner as

instruction in other subject areas. Nearly two decades later, in 1946, the Department of Religion was founded in accordance with this policy.

The establishment of the Department of Religion was accomplished largely through the efforts of two men: President Frank Porter Graham, under whose leadership the Department came into existence, and Mr. James A. Gray, who made funds available to the University for teaching in the area of Bible. Mr. Gray, an alumnus of the University, a long time member of the Board of Trustees, a distinguished and successful businessman, and a trustee of the short lived Chapel Hill School of Religion, had long been interested in the study of the Bible for its own sake, and in 1946 he established a foundation, part of the income of which was to be used as salary for the James A. Gray Professorship of Bible. This was subsequently changed to Biblical Literature.

On the initiative of President Graham, and with the approval of a faculty committee, Dr. Arnold Nash, well known English and American leader in religion in higher education, was appointed Professor of the History of Religion in 1946, and was given the task of developing the Department of Religion. He was joined one year later by Dr. Bernhard W. Anderson, who was appointed Associate Professor of Biblical Literature on the James A. Gray Foundation.

Professor Nash, who had taken graduate degrees in such divergent fields as chemistry, philosophy, and sociology, was especially concerned with the nature of the scientific method and its use in relationship to the natural and social sciences, history, and theology. His book on *The University and the Modern World* ("Essays in the Philosophy of University Education")[2] gives some indication of his orientation, and provides a clue to his understanding of the nature and role of theology and of the study of religion in the university. Addressing himself to the university community in general, Nash argued that "the liberal *Weltanschauung,* based upon the premise that science is presuppositionless and deals with facts and not values," is illusory. On the contrary, he pointed out that every academic endeavor has its presuppositions, and every scholar and teacher his "biases." What Nash called for then, was a recognition of this reality and the acceptance of the need to develop a "new frame of reference in terms of which scientific knowledge can be ordered and understood." Turning to the Christian community in particular, Nash argued for the "the creation of a Christian *speculum mentis . . . ,*" a

Christian world view within which the conclusions of the specialized subjects of the university curriculum could be given their
ultimate meaning in terms of a specifically Christian philosophy
of man and of his relation to the historical process.

Among the tasks which Nash urged upon "Christian scholars" were
(1) applying "Christian criteria in working out the presuppositions
which are relevant to the study of individual academic subjects . . . ,"
and (2) working toward an "intellectual synthesis for the twentieth
century . . . ."

While expressing some scorn for the traditional academic theologian,
whose concern has been too narrow and whose approach too parochial
and unimaginative, Nash did hold that theology, understood as
"man's attempt to understand God's self-revelation . . . , must have its
place in any future *speculum mentis* . . . ." But he stressed that, while
"there will always be need for the critical study of the Bible as the
record of God's revelation . . . ," theology must also "be related to
and be illumined by the wider setting of man's knowledge of the
universe in which it will occupy its appropriate position but also to
which it gives ultimate meaning."

Nash's understanding of theology as a relational discipline found
expression in the two-fold emphasis which characterized the curricular
program in religion at North Carolina in its early stages. On the one
hand, a number of the course offerings were concerned with the
Western religious (and particularly Christian) heritage. These included courses in Biblical history, literature, and theology, and in
aspects of the history of Christian thought. On the other hand, other
courses dealt with "the implications of Christianity for the thought
and practice of today" in an effort to relate "the study of religion
to other fields of learning" and to "help to integrate, in terms of
Christian insights, the knowledge that a student acquires in the various
subjects of study . . ." in the university.[3]

This two-fold orientation has continued to be characteristic of the
Department. This is evidenced by the departmental course offerings,
which in 1963-64 included The Origin and Significance of the Bible;
Introduction to Old Testament Literature; Introduction to New
Testament Literature; The Religions of the World; Varieties of
Religion in American Life and Culture; Christianity and Interpreta-
tions of History; The Relations between Science and Religion; Re-
ligion and Higher Education; Sociology of Religion; and Religious
Art in the West; by the two distinct majors in the Department, one

in Biblical Studies and the other in Religion and Culture; and by the areas of faculty specialization, i.e., Biblical literature, the history and sociology of religion, the role of religion in American culture, and religion and art. Course offerings in recent years, and to a degree from the very beginnings of the Department, have clustered about the two foci of Biblical Studies and of Religion and Culture. The second focus has broadened over the years as seen, for example, in changes in course titles from "Christianity and the Religions of the World" to "The Religions of the World," and from "Christianity and Education" to "Religion and Higher Education"; in the dropping of a course on "The Christian Interpretation of History" and the addition of another course on "Christianity and Interpretations of History"; and in the recent addition of courses dealing with religion and art. This broadening of focus is also evident in a recent departmental analysis which indicates that the "major objective" of the Department is "an examination of the role of religion in the whole of human culture" and which tends accordingly to play down the specific emphasis upon Christianity which characterized early departmental statements of objectives.[4]

Undergraduate concentration in religion has been possible since the establishment of the Department. As indicated above, there are actually two majors offered by the Department according to its most recent listings.[5] One of these, in Biblical Studies, requires six upper-college courses which must include Introduction to Old Testament Literature; Introduction to New Testament Literature; Religion and Culture in Western Civilization; and at least one of the following: The Biblical Perspective; The Work of the Deuteronomists. The other major, in Religion and Culture, requires six upper-college courses which must include Christian Ethics and Modern Problems; Religion and Culture in Western Civilization; and at least one of the following: Religion and Higher Education; Sociology of Religion.

Early statements of the Department indicated that programs "leading to the degrees of M.A. and Ph.D. will be proposed in the near future." Such programs did not exist as of the Spring of 1964. However, it has been possible almost from the beginnings of the Department for a graduate student in another department to take a minor in religion. Thus, students with majors in fields as diverse as art, philosophy, English, sociology and anthropology, radio, television and motion pictures, library science, education, and political science have minored in religion.

In 1950, on Dr. Anderson's departure for seminary teaching, Dr. Bernard Boyd was appointed James A. Gray Professor of Biblical Literature. Dr. Nash subsequently joined the graduate faculty of the Department of Sociology and his title was amended to "Professor of the History and Sociology of Religion." In 1963-64 the Department of Religion had a four-man staff with an assistant professor and an associate professor on the faculty—both paid out of regular University funds—in addition to Professors Boyd and Nash. Three teaching and/or grading assistants were also on the staff of the Department, two paid out of regular University funds—administered through the Graduate School—and one paid from private sources.

Throughout the years of the Department's existence other courses of direct relevance to the study of religion have continued to be offered by other departments. In recent years these have included such courses as The Literary Aspects of the Bible (the Old Testament and the New Testament being taken up in alternate years), in the English Department; Archaeology of the Bible, in the Classics Department; Philosophy of Religion, in the Philosophy Department; and Anthropology of Religion, in the Department of Sociology and Anthropology. In addition to these, Sociology of Religion has been listed in both Religion and Sociology and Anthropology. Furthermore, with the addition of Professor Gerhard Lenski to the Department of Sociology and Anthropology in the Fall of 1963, additional work in the Sociology of Religion will undoubtedly be offered in that Department. Certain relevant courses in languages have also been offered in various language departments, including Greek New Testament, in Classics, and Elementary Hebrew, in the Semitics section of Romance Languages.

In the early years of the Department of Religion, when there were only one or two full-time faculty members in the Department, these and other relevant courses were listed and described among its offerings as well as being listed in their respective departmental descriptions. More recently, as the departmental offerings as such have become more numerous, these extra-departmental courses have been dropped from the Religion listings, but special mention is made of "other undergraduate courses which have a particular relevance to the study of religion," including Philosophy of Religion; Literary Aspects of the Bible; Archaeology of the Bible; and The Ancient Near East (offered in History).[6] There is no obvious formal mechanism, outside or beyond the Department of Religion, for relating or co-ordinating the various courses of relevance to the study of religion.

Departmental Status

As a relative newcomer among the departments of the University, and also just because it represented a subject which generally has to labor against a fair amount of opposition in the university environment, the Department of Religion may have encountered some difficulties in gaining wide acceptance among faculty and administration. Whether the understanding of the Department's basic task as being a relational one may have had any part in stimulating such reservations is not clear. Such a conception could be interpreted, or misinterpreted, as expressing a kind of imperialistic drive which sees religion as the key to understanding the various university disciplines. While the Department was not instituted in an entirely *ad hoc* fashion, general faculty approval of its establishment was neither sought nor gained. However, the first and subsequent appointments to the faculty of the Department have all been made in accordance with standard procedures. There may have hovered about the Department in its early years a certain atmosphere of *noblesse oblige* due to the important role in its founding played by the then President of the University. Perhaps in part because of these circumstances, and certainly also due to a variety of other factors—such as the departure from the University of President Graham shortly after the founding of the Department—it did face difficult going in the first decade or so of its existence. Even today it is the only department in the College of Arts and Sciences not offering graduate degrees.

The status of the Department has been of sufficient concern to its faculty that, at the request of the departmental faculty, a general faculty committee was appointed three years ago to study the role and the future of the Department in particular, and the curricular program in religion in general. This committee had not submitted a formal report by the Fall of 1963. But, in a sense, the fact that at that time a fourth appointment was made to the faculty of the Department could be interpreted as a clear indication of the certainty of the Department's status and future. Further evidence of the Department's status can be seen in the fact that two members of its faculty of four have received in recent years the coveted Tanner Award for "inspirational undergraduate teaching"; in recent appointments of members of the departmental faculty to membership on various important faculty committees; in the acceptance by the appropriate faculty committee of several new courses proposed by the Department; and in the promotion to a tenured position and rank (associate professor) of the youngest member of the departmental faculty.

Enrollment figures indicate that the Department of Religion did not and has not faced difficulties in acceptance among students. Indeed, this Department has had one of the largest enrollments relative to size of faculty of any department in the University, with a ratio of 210 students per instructor in the Spring of 1964 compared with a University average of less than 100 students per instructor. There were 841 enrollments in twelve courses in the Department in that semester, 812 in courses open to undergraduates only (primarily sophomore and up), and twenty-nine in three courses open to upper-classmen and graduate students. There were also twenty-one majors in religion. (See Table VI.)

Courses

The most recent departmental statement (1963-64) [7] suggests that students who wish to study religion "as a major factor in the life of man" might "initially pursue their interest in this field with a consideration of Biblical literature . . . or of the role of religion in American culture . . . or of comparative religion." Accordingly, three introductory courses have been offered in these areas: The Origin and Significance of the Bible; The Varieties of Religion in American Life and Culture; and The Religions of the World. The first of these, which has been taught by Professor Boyd, has consistently had the highest enrollments over the years. It is a course which is designed to view the Bible, and especially the Old Testament, in its historical and religious setting. Students are reminded of the pre-scientific, Oriental, and essentially religious nature of the text. The history of the people of the Old Testament is examined from their ethnic origins in Sumer down to the Exilic and post-Exilic periods. Heavy emphasis is placed on reading from the text, and especially the historical materials in the text.

The course on The Varieties of Religion in American Life and Culture, taught by Associate Professor Samuel S. Hill, Jr., consists of first, an examination of "what Protestantism is, what Roman Catholicism is, what Judaism is"; and second, an effort "to see these three classic faiths in their American setting, noting how they have been affected by the American culture." Some attention is given to the "diversity within these faiths, especially the denominations of

TABLE VI

Enrollments in Selected Courses in Religion: University of North Carolina*

Year and Semester

Course	1956-57 I	1956-57 II	1958-59 I	1958-59 II	1960-61 I	1960-61 II	1961-62 I	1961-62 II	1962-63 I	1962-63 II	1963-64 I	1963-64 II
Origin and Significance of Bible 28	294	252	88	188	168	109	100	220	232	253	210	200
Religious Background of Western Civilization 30			51	11								56
Varieties of Religion in American Life & Culture 32					33	65	60	103	106	149	127	157
" 32A												28
Religions of World 45	75	71	61	34	98	118	111	105	159	197	190	102
Religious Thought in Twentieth Century 75									24		34	28
Intro. to Old Testament Literature 80	8	27	27		59	6	51		67		90	
Intro. to New Testament Literature 81	35	6	40	88		90		103		124		207
Christian Ethics and Modern Problems 91				27	27	56	33	39	37		44	
Christianity and Interpretations of History 93						11		21		33	15	33
Relations between Science and Religion 95							6					
Honors 97, 198												1
Christianity and Education 103	10					8	4		7			1
Biblical Perspective 121				27		13		20	16	17		13
Religion and Culture in Western Civilization 130				3		8		8		17		15
Sociology of Religion 170				8		11		15		28	15	
Work of Deuteronomists 171						9		9		13		13

Totals in Department of Religion

	1956-57 I	1956-57 II	1958-59 I	1958-59 II	1960-61 I	1960-61 II	1961-62 I	1961-62 II	1962-63 I	1962-63 II	1963-64 I	1963-64 II
By semester	422	434	238	358	394	494	374	630	645	818	738	841
For the year	856		596		888		1004		1463		1579	
Eng. 63, Literary Aspects of Bible				25		21		27		18		15
Phil. 52, Philosophy of Religion	51	71	46	67	75	93	62	55	97	78	91	99
Phil. 208, Philosophy of Religion				14								
Anthrop. 123, Anthropology of Religion	5			22				23				63

* Enrollment figures supplied by the Department of Religion.

Protestantism and the divisions of Judaism." Nearly one-third of the course is concerned with "the history of religion in America, since religion in contemporary America . . . cannot be understood without such a study." In sum, the three major faiths and "American religion in general" are studied "from historical, theological, and sociological standpoints." The required textbooks in this course include: Brown, *The Spirit of Protestantism;* Baeck, *Essence of Judaism;* Adam, *The Spirit of Catholicism;* Olmstead, *Religion in America: Past and Present;* and Herberg, *Protestant, Catholic, Jew.*

The course on The Religions of the World, taught by Professor Nash, is not entirely typical of courses with this title offered at some institutions in that substantial attention is given to a consideration of three "modern religions"—"Scienticity," Communism, and Nationalism. Assigned or suggested readings include: selections from the *Life* magazine series on "The World's Great Religions"; selections from the Koran, the "Path of Dharma," and the "Tripitaka"; Smith, *The Religions of Man;* Julian Huxley, *The Faith of a Humanist;* A. C. Benjamin, *Science and its Presuppositions;* Lundberg, *Can Science Save Us?* Standen, *Science Is a Sacred Cow;* John Bennett, "The Nature of Communism"; Mendel, ed., *Essential Works of Marxism;* Crossman, ed., *The God That Failed;* Waugh, "Death in Hollywood," *Life* magazine, 9-29-47; Sargeant, "Cult of the Love Goddess in America," *Life* magazine, 11-10-47; Hamill, *Gods of the Campus;* Walsh, *Campus Gods on Trial;* Pittenger, "Christianity and Americanism"; Commager, "Our Schools Have Kept Us Free"; F. C. Grant, "The World View of the Old Testament"; Loew, *Modern Rivals to Christian Faith;* Trueblood, "The New Comparative Religion"; and selected writings by Professor Nash.

Other courses listed by the Department of Religion include:

For undergraduates—

The Religious Background of Western Civilization
Impact of the faith of the Old Testament, Graeco-Roman religion, Teutonic religion, and Christianity upon the life and thought of the Western World.

Religious Thought in the Twentieth Century
Recent trends in religious thought as exhibited in thinkers like Reinhold Niebuhr, Jacques Maritain, Martin Buber, Paul Tillich, and William Temple.

Introduction to Old Testament Literature

Introduction to New Testament Literature

Christian Ethics and Modern Problems

Christianity and Interpretations of History
Biblical, liberal protestant, and other Christian interpretations of history as compared to such secular views as the Marxist, the progressivist, and the nihilist.

The Relations Between Science and Religion
The mutual influence of natural science and religion upon each other in Western civilization since 1500.

Courses for Honors.

For graduates and advanced undergraduates —

The Biblical Perspective
Central themes of the Bible, and the tension between the Biblical *Weltanschauung* and other world views.

Religion and Culture in Western Civilization
Relationships between the religions of the Western World and the different cultural expressions which these religions have taken.

Sociology of Religion
Tensions between scientific, ethical and theological study of society; role of religion in social change; social origins of the denominations; sociological significance of the Reformation; "sect" and "church" in sociological theory.

The Work of the Deuteronomists
Their philosophy of history, their continuity with the prophetic movement, and their contributions to the development of Biblical thought.

Four new courses were approved by the faculty of the College of Arts and Sciences for addition to the Departmental offerings in 1964: For undergraduates —

The Religious Imagination in the Ancient World
Basic principles of the religious imagination; the several foundations of Western culture studied through its imaginative manifestation in literature, art, and forms of worship.

For graduates and advanced undergraduates —

The Religious Element in the American Tradition

Interaction of American religious institutions and concepts with the dominant ideas, movements, and values in the American tradition.

The Religious Imagination in the Medieval and Modern World

Religious imagination in selected manifestations in literature, art, and types of worship, from the Middle Ages to the present.

Religious Art in the West

Origins of religious art in faith and formal liturgy, and the impact of artistic development on the life and thought of religious institutions.

This last course will also be listed in Art. Three of these new courses have been designed by Dr. John W. Dixon, Jr., specialist in religion and art, who was appointed Associate Professor of Religion in the Fall of 1963.

Conclusions

It is evident that these courses, together with relevant courses offered in other departments, offer the student a wide variety from which to choose and afford him an opportunity to study religion from a number of approaches, including historical, sociological, anthropological, literary, philosophical, and theological approaches. Altogether, the curricular program in religion is a quite impressive one, especially at the undergraduate level, and enrollments indicate a substantial interest in the subject.

The present disposition of the Department seems to be one of moving in the direction of the appointment of scholars with specialties in the relationship between religion and some other academic area —such as art, as in the case of Professor Dixon, or psychology, which has been suggested as a desirable relational area for the next appointment to the Department. This continual movement in a "bridge" or relational direction is entirely in keeping with the early departmental emphasis on relating the study of religion to other fields of learning. It offers the obvious advantage of strengthening ties with other academic areas which may engage in the study of religion and of engaging in the study of this complex field on a broad scale. It also may be of some strategic value in strengthening the status and the "image" of this relatively new Department. More importantly, the appointment to the faculty of men genuinely competent in "bridge areas" and thoroughly conversant with developments in two fields can contribute significantly to the intellectual exchange or "dialogue" which is a necessary component in the university community and which becomes progressively more difficult to achieve as that community becomes more complex and segmented. There is no doubt that the presence of the Department of Religion at the University of North Carolina—and specifically of a faculty with broad intellectual interests and concerns—has had some influence upon the intellectual life of that University. It is difficult for the outside observer to judge the exact nature and extent of that influence, but it is clear that the Department of Religion has made its presence felt both among students and faculty. It has avoided the temptation to become an intellectual ghetto—a temptation which lures all academic departments and is perhaps especially strong among departments of religion.

It seems to this observer that one of the major necessities confronting the Department is the fuller development of specialized and advanced study in religion. The fact that this is the one department in the College of Arts and Sciences which does not offer a program leading to a graduate degree or degrees suggests that the Department is underdeveloped. Perhaps it points also to the difficulties—both theoretical and practical—involved in structuring a department of religion in which advanced scholarly study can take place. The field is very broad. Areas of specialization are greatly varied. And various disciplines can be utilized in the study of religion. The relational or bridge approach to religion—which has been stressed at the University of North Carolina—does recognize the complexity of the subject and the fact that various disciplines quite naturally concern themselves with it. But the implications of this approach for the development of systematic and specialized study of religion are not entirely clear since it is an approach which leaves unanswered the question of a common core or focal point for specialized study as well as the related question of the nature and development of the discipline or disciplines centrally concerned with the direct study of religion.

Another way of describing a problem which is not unique to the Department of Religion at the University of North Carolina is to point out that there is little opportunity for giving direct attention to methodology in the study of religion. Such attention is not necessary to, and perhaps would be superfluous in a curricular program which emphasizes breadth and is designed to appeal primarily to students who are specializing in some other area. But concern with methodology —with the tools and methods of research and the definition and delimitation of subject matter—does appear to be a necessity to fruitful specialization.

Biographical and Bibliographical Information about Faculty in the Department of Religion; the University of North Carolina

BERNARD BOYD, *James A. Gray Professor of Biblical Literature*

B. 1910. Presbyterian College, A.B.; Princeton Theological Seminary, Th.B.; Princeton University, M.A.; Union Theological Seminary, Virginia, Th.D.

Teaching Positions: Presbyterian College, 1936-1946; Davidson College, 1947-1950; The University of North Carolina, 1950-; Chairman, Department of Religion, The University of North Carolina, 1952-1960.

Engaged in educational television.

Recipient of Tanner Award for Distinction in College Teaching, The University of North Carolina.

JOHN W. DIXON, JR., *Associate Professor*

B. 1919. Emory and Henry College, B.A.; University of Chicago (Committee on Social Thought), Ph.D.

Teaching Positions: Michigan State College, 1950-52; Emory University, 1952-57; Dickinson College, 1957-60; Florida Presbyterian College, 1960-63; The University of North Carolina, 1963-.

Author: Form and Reality: Art as Communication, 1957; *Nature and Grace in Art* (forthcoming by University of North Carolina Press) ; articles.

SAMUEL S. HILL, JR., *Associate Professor*

B. 1927. Georgetown College, A.B.; Vanderbilt University, M.A. (English) ; Southern Baptist Theological Seminary, B.D.; Duke University, Ph.D.

Teaching Positions: Stetson University, 1959-60; The University of North Carolina, 1960-. Chairman, Department of Religion, The University of North Carolina, 1961-.

Author: Articles; *Baptists—North and South,* with Robert G. Torbet, 1964. Recipient of Tanner award for Distinction in College Teaching, The University of North Carolina.

ARNOLD NASH, *Professor of the History and Sociology of Religion*
B. 1906. Education at University of Liverpool, Ripon Hall, Oxford,
and the London School of Economics, University of London.
Has lectured at various American universities and been a member
of the faculties of the Church Divinity School of the Pacific and
McCormick Theological Seminary. Chairman, Department of
Religion, The University of North Carolina, 1946-1952.

Editor and contributor to *Education for Christian Marriage,* 1940,
and of *Protestant Thought in the Twentieth Century,* 1951;
author, *The University and the Modern World* (cited above)
and numerous scholarly articles and monographs.

*Biographical Information on Staff Members who Teach
Courses Cross-Listed with Religion*   .

A. C. HOWELL, *Professor of English*
Denison, A.B.; Columbia, M.A.; The University of North Carolina,
Ph.D.
Teaching at The University of North Carolina since 1920.

MAURICE NATANSON, *Professor of Philosophy*
Lincoln Memorial, A.B.; New York University, M.A.; The University
of Nebraska, Ph.D.; The New School for Social Research,
D.S.Sc.
Teaching at The University of North Carolina since 1957.

JOHN J. HONIGMANN, *Professor of Anthropology and Research Professor*
Brooklyn College A.B., M.A.; Yale University, Ph.D.
Teaching at The University of North Carolina since 1951.

---

1. For a fuller account of the events of the 1920's, see *The University of North
Carolina, 1900-1930,* Louis R. Wilson (Chapel Hill, The University of North Carolina Press, 1957) pp. 537-546. Quotation from p. 545.

2. (New York, The Macmillan Co., 1944.) Quotations that follow are from chapters
6 and 7.

3. Quotations from the "Provisional Statement" on the Department of Religion,
the University of North Carolina Record, The General Catalogue for the 154th
Session, 1947-48, and the General Catalogue for the Long Session, 1949-50.

4. In the "Self-Study Summary Report," the University of North Carolina at
Chapel Hill, January 15, 1964, pp. 96-98.

5. *The University of North Carolina Record, The General Catalogue Issue,*
1963-64, pp. 245 ff.

6. *Ibid.*

7. *Ibid.* Course descriptions from this source, and from course outlines and
syllabi.

VI

A PROGRAM IN COMPARATIVE RELIGION AND AN INDEPENDENT SCHOOL OF RELIGION:

Indiana University

History and Rationale

Various features of the curricular program in religion at Indiana University make it of special interest to this study. It stresses, by its name at least, "Comparative Religion." It is not departmental in nature; the majority of courses listed in the Program are offered in existing departments in the College of Arts and Sciences. However, some of the courses listed are offered only under the rubric "Comparative Religion" and thus have no departmental base. These particular courses have been taught by faculty members in the Indiana School of Religion, a private corporation with no formal structural relationship to the University. One of these individuals has had a position of professorial rank in the University while the others have had the status of lecturers. Thus the Program has been developed chiefly by the use of two devices, the listing of relevant courses offered in existing departments, and the inclusion of other courses taught by qualified instructors from the independent, off-campus School of Religion. Some of these latter courses were based on non-credit courses which had been offered in the Indiana School of Religion before the institution of the Program in Comparative Religion.

The Program in Comparative Religion was instituted in 1953 under the leadership of Dr. John W. Ashton, who was then Vice-President and Dean of Student and Educational Services and has since become Dean of the Graduate School and Vice-President for Graduate Development. Dean Ashton became Chairman of the Executive Committee in charge of the Program, a Committee made up of selected faculty members appointed by the Dean of the College of Arts and Sciences, and remained in that position until September 1961 when he was replaced as Chairman by Professor Roy Battenhouse of the Department of English. As indicated, in the decade of its existence the Committee has utilized two devices in the development of the Program: (1) the encouraging and listing of relevant courses in various departments, and (2) the appointment of Indiana School of Religion faculty members as lecturers to teach courses which have been listed only under the rubric of "Comparative Religion." A significant step was taken in

1961 with the appointment of Dr. Henry Fischel, scholar in Hebrew and Judaic studies, as Associate Professor of Asian Studies in the University. Dr. Fischel was also appointed Associate Professor in the Indiana School of Religion. Part of his salary has come from University sources and part from the Indiana School of Religion.

The Executive Committee in charge of the Indiana Program in Comparative Religion has argued that "in any effort to understand a culture or area of the world, past or present, religion is a factor whose importance it would be difficult to overstress."[1] It has urged further that "no college or university can offer a truly adequate educational program without including an intelligent consideration of religious history and content." Thus there has been no question in the mind of the Committee regarding the importance of the area and the desirability and necessity of its study. The questions of approach, organization, and manner of study have not been as easily handled as has the question of the legitimacy of study. While the term "comparative religion" is used, the Committee has not spelled out its meaning and the curricular listings under the heading of Comparative Religion do not give much of a clue as to that meaning. One has the impression that the designation was chosen because in present-day university circles it suggests academic legitimacy and concern with more than one culture. In any case, the designation has obviously not meant to the Committee what it sometimes meant a generation or two ago when "comparative religion" carried the suggestion in some circles that such a method could be employed to indicate the superiority of one religion over others.

From its beginnings the Committee has stressed the study of religion as an aspect of liberal arts. "Even as an understanding of religious values and attitudes is a necessary part of education in the broad sense," the Committee has argued, "so special interest in religion is best pursued within the framework of a liberal education which brings the student into contact with the concepts of man, society, and the universe." In this connection the Committee has called special attention to the close tie of the study of religion with the humanities while also indicating that "the social implications of religion are ever-present in the social sciences . . . ."

At various times the Committee has (*a*) suggested the outline of an ideal curriculum in religion, (*b*) given considerable thought to questions of approach and what is involved in the direct study of religion, (*c*) surveyed relevant course offerings at Indiana and departmental sentiments concerning further development of studies in religion, and (*d*) surveyed curricular programs in religion at other Big Ten institutions. A recent report of the Committee on Comparative Religion (ca. 1960) made in connection with a request for recommendations from the General Committee on Indiana University in Relation to World Affairs, suggested that the ideal curriculum in Comparative Religion might include the following:

Introductory:

(1) A two-semester introduction to the religions of East and West.

Three Principal Areas of Study:

(2) Religious thought and theology, including philosophy of religion, Christian thought at the various chronological stages, Hebrew-Jewish, Moslem, Indian, Buddhist, and Chinese philosophy or thought.

(3) The history of religion, including both Western and Eastern.

(4) The literature of religion, including the method of interpreting religious documents, analysis of religious themes and myths, and the study of selected religious literature expressing various traditions.

More Specialized Areas:

(5) The sociology of religion.

(6) The psychology of religion.

(7) Religious media of communication (drama, music, art, and religious symbols).

The report listed existing courses of relevance and suggested that "ideally the program should have a scholar teacher for each of the major religions besides Christianity." To this end, the report suggested the desirability of the addition of specialists in Moslem religion and culture, Buddhism, the religions of China and Japan, and Indian sects and religions, and of adequate funds for library and other resources to aid these specialists in their work. The report concluded that "if the Program in Comparative Religion is to have the significance it deserves, it might well plan to have a staff composed of scholars whose major interest would be in the various religions of the world."

More recently (December, 1963) the Executive Committee on Comparative Religion recommended to the Dean of the College of Arts and Sciences the appointment of a Professor or an Associate Professor who would be assigned the task of organizing an integrated program in "religious studies" in the general area of the humanities, the primary aim of which would be to provide students with an opportunity to learn something about the complex religious situation of contemporary culture. In making this recommendation, the Committee pointed to the "manifold and intricate theological and religious issues of the present day" and suggested that these are "matters that lend themselves to such disciplined treatment and investigation as are appropriate to an academic institution." One interesting aspect of this recommendation, when compared with the earlier report of the Committee discussed above, is the more obvious recognition of "a discipline in areas that may in a rather more proper sense be termed religious and theological" as well as the continuing acknowledgment of the importance to any program of studies in religion of relevant study in such related disciplines as history, anthropology, sociology, literature, and philosophy.

In a recently issued report "concerning actual and potential course offerings" at Indiana "that could be considered relevant to a Program in Religious Studies" the Committee indicated that there are quite a number of such courses offered in various departments. The "problems," the Committee suggested, however,

> has never been one of a lack of offerings, but rather one of whether and how a very heterogeneous array of courses drawn from very divergent areas could ever be integrated into a program of studies in religion that could, with some slight meaning and some semblance of justification, be regarded as an ordered program of work for an undergraduate student.

The Committee suggested further that "none of the course offerings" presently in existence in the various departments "might be said to be courses in religion proper." (The Committee did not include in its survey courses presently offered *only* under the rubric "Comparative Religion." Presumably these might fit the Committee's definition of "courses in religion proper.") It was against this kind of background that the Committee apparently decided to recommend the appointment of a faculty member who would be assigned the task of developing an ordered program by relating various courses already offered and by facilitating the addition of courses which would deal directly with religion.

Present Curriculum

Courses listed under "Comparative Religion" in the 1963-64 catalogue of the College of Arts and Sciences include seven offered only under that program, that is, courses which are not listed or offered by one of the departments; and thirty-one courses offered in such departments and programs as Anthropology, Classics, Comparative Literature, English, Fine Arts, French and Italian, History, Linguistics, Music, Philosophy, and Sociology. Courses listed only in Comparative Religion include Introduction to World Religions I-II, The Church in the Middle Ages, History of Christian Thought I-II, Old Testament Times, and The Christian Church in New Testament Times. All of these courses were approved by the Curriculum Committee of the College of Arts and Sciences before their introduction into the Program.

Introduction to World Religions is offered in two separate units of three semester hours each. India and the Far East are dealt with in one unit which includes discussions of primitive religion, representative national religions, early Hinduism, Jainism, Buddhism in its first phase, the religious development of Buddhism, later Hinduism, Sikhism, Chinese religion and the Taoists, Confucianism, and Shinto. The other unit of the course is devoted to a discussion of the religions of the West, including national religions of the past, the Persian and Hebrew backgrounds and the later development of Judaism, the development of Christianity (Protestantism and Roman Catholicism), and the beginnings and development of Islam. The text for both units is Noss, *Man's Religions*.[2]

The students are also given a list of supplementary readings and a number of guide questions to aid them in their reading of Noss. This course has been taught by various members of the staff at the Indiana School of Religion. It was developed primarily by Dr. Harold Hill. Beginning in the Fall of 1963, and on the recommendation of the Committee on Comparative Religion and the Curriculum Committee, Introduction to World Religions I and II were accepted by the faculty of the College of Arts and Sciences as options which might be chosen by students to meet one of the College requirements for the A.B. degree. Comparative Religion C-153-C154 (Introduction to World Religions I-II) is listed, thus, as an option along with offerings in such areas as Comparative Literature, Classics, Fine Arts,

Speech and Theatre, Philosophy, and various language courses with a literary content.

The Church in the Middle Ages offers a study of the Church from the eighth through the fifteenth centuries, gives attention to historical, cultural, and religious developments in the Western and Eastern churches and places special emphasis upon evaluation of doctrinal and institutional influences as they affected medieval Christianity. The text used during 1962-63—the only year this course has been offered thus far—was Philip Hughes, *A History of the Church,* vol. 2. The course was taught by Dr. William J. H. Price, who was at that time Lecturer in Indiana University and Associate Professor of Christian Thought in the Indiana School of Religion.

The History of Christian Thought, taught by Dr. D. J. Bowden (Lecturer in Indiana University and Professor of Christian Thought and Director of the Indiana School of Religion since 1953), is a study of the rise and development of fundamental beliefs in the history of Christianity. The first semester (three hours) is devoted to the period up to the Reformation era, and the second semester (three hours also) to modern Christian thought from the Reformation to the present. The revised edition of Williston Walker, *A History of the Christian Church,* is used as a text. In addition the students are given extended syllabi and are assigned outside readings in such authors as Augustine and Thomas Aquinas during the first semester and in Bainton, *Here I Stand;* Schleiermacher, *On Religion: Speeches to Its Cultured Despisers;* and Tillich, *Dynamics of Faith* in the second.

Old Testament Times, taught by Dr. Hill, is a two-semester hour course which deals with the cultural milieu of the ancient Near East as related to the roots of Judaism, Christianity and Islam. Assigned readings include selections from the Hebrew Bible or Old Testament and Anderson, *Understanding the Old Testament.* The Christian Church in New Testament Times is also a two-semester hour course taught by Dr. Hill which deals with the beginnings of Christianity, especially in the first century. Sources include the Acts of the Apostles, the Letters of Paul, James, Peter, Jude and John. The text is Kee and Young, *Understanding the New Testament.*

An analysis of the courses listed only under "Comparative Religion" indicates that they are almost all of an introductory or survey type. None of them requires previous work in the field. These courses are of a "service" nature and are not part of a concentration program.

(A major or graduate degrees are not offered in "Comparative Religion.") Students with a wide variety of interests and backgrounds enroll in them. A study of the career intentions of students enrolled in these courses in 1962-63 indicated the following distribution: medical science, 18.5 per cent; education, 17.1; business, 12; nursing, 10.6; housewife, 7.4; law, 6.8; ministry, 4.1; social service, 2.8; dentistry, 1.6; speech and hearing therapy, 1.6; physical therapy, 1.4; other, 7.8; and undecided, 7.3.

Departmental courses which are also listed under "Comparative Religion" include:

Primitive Religion, in Anthropology

Classical Mythology; Christian Classics I: Augustine to Bunyan; Christian Classics II: Pascal to Eliot; and Development of Hebrew Literature and Thought—Post-Biblical I-II-III; in Comparative Literature

Milton; and Literature of the Bible I-II; in English

Early Medieval Art; Romanesque and Gothic Art; The Art of Persia, India, and Southeast Asia; in Fine Arts

Dante; in French and Italian

History of Ancient Civilization I-II-III; The Reformation; Medieval History, 200-1400 I-II; in History

A three-year sequence in Hebrew; in Linguistics

Church Music I-II; and Seminar in Liturgics and Hymnology; in Music

Ethics and Philosophy of Religion; in Philosophy

The Sociology of Political and Religious Movements; in Sociology

The courses in Christian Classics and Literature of the Bible are taught by Professor Roy Battenhouse, who has a theological degree as well as a Ph.D. degree in English. The Literature of the Bible has been a standard offering in the Indiana English Department for many years. The required textbook for the course is *The Dartmouth Bible*, edited by Chamberlain and Feldman. Auxiliary books are used for various special purposes. The first semester covers virtually everything in *The Dartmouth Bible* up to the Old Testament Apocrypha. The second semester begins with the "Intertestamental" literature and proceeds through the Gospels, the Book of Acts and several of the Pauline Epistles. The approach in the course is described by Professor Battenhouse as being "literary-historical-theological." However, the literary is primary, in that the chief focus is on the structure and styling of individual stories and of the respective books making up the Bible.

Philosophy of Religion is taught by Distinguished Service Professor Henry Veatch. Topics discussed include the following: natural theology; the general issue of religion and philosophy; mystical religion; the "Existentialist" ferment in contemporary religious thought; types of "apologiae" for religion; the question of religious language; the import of religion as regards human society, history and culture; and the psychology and phenomenology of religion. No single textbook is used in the course, but extensive use is made of readings from primary sources.

The courses in Hebrew Language and Literature are taught by Dr. Henry Fischel, who is Associate Professor of Asian studies in the College of Arts and Sciences and Associate Professor of Judaic Studies in the Indiana School of Religion. Development of Hebrew Literature and Thought, Post-Biblical, is offered in a three-semester sequence. The first semester is devoted to the origin, nature and development of Rabbinic Judaism and its relationships with other religious currents and movements. The second semester is concerned with subsequent developments up to the twentieth century, including such subjects as the revival of philosophy and its fusion with medieval belief, "the afterlife of the talmudic method," the development of mysticism and the role of esoterics, the impact of the Renaissance and the Enlightenment, the rise of nationalism and Chassidism, and the regrouping and reformulation of the Hebraic-Judaic civilization in the nineteenth century. The third semester brings these developments to the present. Readings are assigned from Baron, *A Social and Religious History of the Jews;* Finkelstein, *The Jews; The Jewish People, Past and Present* (Jewish Encyclopedia Handbooks); Waxman, *A History of Jewish Literature;* and a number of additional relevant works. Enrollments in these and other courses in "Comparative Religion" are listed in Table VII.

The Indiana School of Religion

While there is no formal structural relationship between Indiana University and the Indiana School of Religion, the faculty of the School has played an important role in the development and teaching of courses in the Comparative Religion Program. During the 1962-63 academic year three members of this faculty (Bowden, Hill and Price) taught courses in Comparative Religion with the status of

TABLE VII

Enrollments in Courses in the Program in Comparative Religion:
Indiana University*

Course	1955-56		1957-58		1960-61		1961-62		1962-63		1963-64	
	I	II	I	II	I	II	I	II	I	II	I	II
Intro. World Religions I ..					25	28	21	34	22	34	69	151
Intro. World Religions II					16	67	35	100	49	123	66	143
Church in Middle Ages									3	4		
History of Christian Thought			11	8	24	30	33	42	22	34	15	33
Old Testament Times	12		12			14		22		20		21
Christian Church in New Testament Times..		12		23	6		14		6		16	
Primitive Religion (Anthropol.)	21			16	26				26			
Classical Mythology (Classics)	28	23	24	45	20	26	37	34			44	46
Christian Classics I-II (Comparative Literature)	6	15	11	13	14	15			10			
Dev. of Hebrew Literature and Thought—Post Biblical I-II-III (Comp. Literature)							4	13	9	14	12	
Milton (English)		25		23		41		42				36
Literature of Bible I-II	18	36	23	28	12	15	25	29	22	21	32	25
Early Medieval Art (Fine Arts)							17		17		14	
Romanesque and Gothic Art (Fine Arts)	18							11		29		14
Art of Persia, India, Southeast Asia (Fine Arts)										14		
Dante (French & Italian) I-II									10	7	6	7
History of Ancient Civilization (History) I-II-III	22	34	53	41	75	46	50	75	30	30	105	75
Reformation (History)		31				23	12			16		
Medieval History, 200-1400, I-II (History)	15	19	16		23	19	36	36	32	40	31	33
Elementary Hebrew I-II (Linguistics)	2				6	7	8	7	9	7	12	10
2nd-yr. Hebrew I-II (Linguistics)							3	3		1	7	6
3rd-yr. Hebrew I-II (Linguistics)									2	2	3	3

(Continued on Next Page)

TABLE VII (*Continued*)

Course	1955-56 I	II	1957-58 I	II	1960-61 I	II	1961-62 I	II	1962-63 I	II	1963-64 I	II
									Year and Semester			
Church Music I-II (Music)	10		6	4	1	3	8	9			12	11
Seminar in Liturgics & Hymnology (Music)† ..												
Ethics (Philosophy)	115	136	112	109	133	167	128	194	107	203	184	126
Philosophy of Religion (Philos.)										81		
Sociology of Political and Religious Movements (Sociol.)		4		28		29		20				

* Enrollment figures supplied by the office of the Graduate Dean.
† Not offered in years listed.

Lecturers and one (Fischel) had professorial status in the University. In recent years the administration and Board of Directors of the School have defined the role of the School as being primarily one of serving the University in the teaching of relevant courses in religion.

The Indiana School of Religion was founded in 1910 as a Disciples of Christ Bible Chair. The name was changed in 1917, and non-credit courses were offered to students of Indiana University, and to others in Bloomington and other Indiana cities. After the creation of the interdepartmental Program in Comparative Religion in the College of Arts and Sciences in the University in 1953, staff members in the School were invited to become lecturers in the University and to teach courses in this Program. In 1953-54, six semester hours were taught in this Program by staff members of the School of Religion. By 1962-63 courses taught in this fashion had expanded to 58 semester hours of offerings.

The Indiana School of Religion is a separate corporation, and up until the Fall of 1963 it had received all of its support from private sources. The major sources of this support have been foundations, corporations, churches and individuals. A new building was constructed in 1956-57 at an approximate cost of $115,000. Of this amount, $37,500 was donated by the Lilly Endowment, Inc., on a matching basis, and $10,000 was given by the Krannert Foundation for equipment. Gifts donated by other individuals, companies and foundations made it possible to complete the project with no indebtedness. A significant step was taken in 1963 when the University agreed to rent the building at a fee of $6,000 for the year. The total operating budget of the School is now over $50,000 per year. Nearly all of this money has been raised by the Director of the School.

Church organizations which have contributed to the operating budget of the School include the Disciples of Christ, the Episcopal Diocese of Indianapolis, the three Methodist Conferences of Indiana, the Presbyterian Synod of Indiana, the Synod of Indiana of the Lutheran Church in America, the South Indiana Synod of the Evangelical and Reformed Church, and the Society of Friends in Bloomington. The appointment of Dr. Henry Fischel was made possible in the Fall of 1961 with the help of a grant from the Hebrew Culture Foundation of New York City and contributions from other Jewish sources. Part of Professor Fischel's salary also comes from University sources. As noted above, in 1963-64 he was the only School of Religion staff member with professorial status in the University and the only one to receive some direct support through the University. In the Fall of 1963 efforts were being made by the School of Religion and the Indiana University Foundation to raise additional sums from Jewish sources in Indiana for the support of Judaic studies in the University. The three-year appointment (Fall 1960 to Spring 1963) of Dr. William J. H. Price, an historical theologian and an ordained Roman Catholic priest, was made possible by a grant of $31,200 from the Lilly Endowment, Inc. It is the intention of the School to make a similar appointment in the near future.

The staff of the School of Religion teaches almost exclusively now in the Program in Comparative Religion. Only one non-credit course was offered in the School in 1962-63. In the past the staff, and especially Professors Bowden and Hill, has devoted considerable time to teaching courses in various extension centers and in churches, as well as in the School itself. Professor Bowden still teaches the History of Christian Thought on the Indianapolis campus—in the Indiana School of Nursing—as well as in the Comparative Religion Program on the Bloomington campus. Pressures have been so great upon the staff of the School that little time has been available for research and writing.

Future directions of the Indiana School of Religion depend to a considerable extent upon developments within the Program in Comparative Religion in the University. It is possible that other members of the staff of the School—in addition to Professor Fischel—may be granted professorial status in the College of Arts and Sciences.[3]

Conclusions

As one attempts to discern the possible patterns of future development of the Program in Comparative Religion in the College of Arts and Sciences of Indiana University, certain questions arise. Will the Program continue as an interdepartmental program under an executive committee or will there be a movement toward the creation of a separate department? In either case, will efforts be made to bring about a more integrated curricular program with provisions for concentrated study at both the undergraduate and graduate levels? If such efforts are made, will the Program be staffed by the appointment to professorial status of the present lecturers from the School of Religion or by the appointment of additional professors or by appointments of both types? If greater opportunity for concentrated study in religion becomes a fact will funds be available for library and other resources needed to sustain the scholarly study of religion? What will be the approach that may inform and guide future developments? Will it be primarily a direct or an indirect approach, one that recognizes the integrity of the field and the disciplines devoted to its direct study or one based upon an indirect study of religion primarily by and through the already existing disciplines in the University? Will the approach be primarily historical and anthropological, or phenomenological, or perhaps even theological in nature? These and similar questions now face the Executive Committee in Comparative Religion, and beyond them, the faculty of the College of Arts and Sciences and the administration of the College and the University.

As it now stands, the Program in Comparative Religion appears to be little more than a device for listing relevant courses in various departments and for offering four or five additional courses which are not offered in the departments. The one thread which gives the Program some semblance of unity is religion—broadly conceived. This has the merit of calling attention to the fact that religion is a vast and complex area. But the systematic study of religion requires more ordering than is obvious in the existing Program at Indiana. The Executive Committee in charge of the Program, as noted above, has been aware of the lack of cohesiveness and direction in the Program and has recommended that steps be taken to remedy this. Specifically, the Committee has recommended the appointment to the faculty of a qualified scholar who would have the rather large task of attempting to bring about this direction and cohesiveness by encouraging more offerings in the study of religion in various departments and by developing further a core program in the direct study of religion.

The Indiana Program in Comparative Religion has benefited considerably from the resources of the Indiana School of Religion— and specifically in its use of the faculty of that institution. For more than a decade faculty members of the independent School of Religion have taught as lecturers in the Program and without stipend from the University. It seems to this observer that the trustees and faculty of the School of Religion have been wise in conceiving of the task of the School as being primarily one of advancing the study of religion in the University. At the same time, it is quite clear that if the Program in Comparative Religion is to develop significantly it should be staffed at its "core" by men of professorial rank who possess the scholarly abilities ordinarily required for such an appointment. This would appear to be a *sine qua non* of policy. How such a policy would be applied—whether, for example, the present lecturers should receive such appointments—is obviously a matter involving administrative decision.

The Indiana Program in Comparative Religion, now in existence for a decade, is interesting in its efforts to develop a broad and scholarly approach to the study of religion in a tax-supported University and in its use of the staff of the independent School of Religion for teaching some of the basic courses in the Program. There is considerable potential in the Program yet to be realized. An institution of the experience and stature of Indiana University could well develop one of the more significant programs in this area in the United States.

Biographical and Bibliographical Information on Selected Faculty and Lecturers Associated with the Indiana Program in Comparative Religion

BATTENHOUSE, ROY WESLEY, *Professor of English*
B. 1912. Albion, B.A. 1933; Yale, B.D. 1936, Ph.D. 1938; Indiana, 1950-.
Interests: Theology of Shakespeare, English religious thought, especially in the Elizabethan period, Renaissance thought, St. Augustine, the tradition of Christian humanistic thought.
Publications: Heavy contributor to journals. Book: *Companion to the Study of St. Augustine,* ed., 1955.

BIDNEY, DAVID, *Professor of Anthropology and Philosophy*

B. 1908. Toronto, B.A. 1928, M.A. 1929; Yale, Ph.D. 1932; Indiana, 1950-.

Interests: Theory of myth, primitive religion, comparative ethics and law, philosophy of Descartes and Spinoza.

Publications: Numerous articles. Books: *Psychology and Ethics of Spinoza*, 1940; *Theoretical Anthropology*, 1953; *The Concept of Freedom in Anthropology*, ed., 1963; *Man's Image in Medicine and Anthropology*, contributor, 1963.

FISCHEL, HENRY HEINZ ALBERT, *Associate Professor of Asian Studies, and in the Indiana School of Religion*

B. 1920. Edinburgh, Ph.D. 1944; Indiana, 1961-.

Interests: Background of the New Testament, Religion, literature and civilization of the Biblical and Hellenistic Near East, Gnosticism among Jews.

Publications: Heavy contributor to journals. Book: *The First Book of Maccabees, Introduction and Commentary*, 1948.

HOGUE, ARTHUR REED, *Associate Professor of History*

B. 1916. Oberlin, B.A. 1928; Harvard, M.A. 1929, Ph.D. 1937; Indiana, 1950-.

Interests: Legal history, European intellectual history, Carl Schurtz, Medieval English law.

Publications: Articles. Book: Carl Schurtz, *Charles Summer: An Essay*, ed.

KIRKPATRICK, CLIFFORD L., *Professor of Sociology*

B. 1898. Clark, B.A. 1920, M.A. 1922; Pennsylvania, Ph.D. 1935; Indiana, 1949-.

Interests: Social psychology, sociology of religion.

Publications: Numerous articles. Book: *Religion in Human Affairs*, 1929.

VEATCH, HENRY BABCOCK, *Distinguished Service Professor of Philosophy*

B. 1911. Harvard, B.A. 1932, M.A. 1933, Ph.D. 1936; Indiana, 1937-.

Interests: Philosophy and religion, metaphysics, realism and nominalism.

Publications: Numerous articles. Books: *Intentional Logic*, 1952; *Realism and Nominalism Revisited*, 1954; *Logic as a Human Instrument*, 1959; *Rational Man*, 1962.

BOWDEN, DANIEL JOSEPH, *Lecturer, Indiana University, and Professor and Director, Indiana School of Religion*

B. 1906. Virginia Polytechnic Institute, B.S. 1928; Yale University, B.D. 1933, Ph.D. 1937; Indiana School of Religion and Lecturer, Indiana University, 1953-.

Publications: Articles.

HILL, HAROLD EUGENE, *Lecturer, Indiana University, and Associate Professor, Indiana School of Religion*

B. 1920. California, B.A. 1942; San Francisco Seminary, B.D. 1945; Yale, Ph.D. 1955; Indiana School of Religion, 1948-; Lecturer, Indiana University, 1953-.

Interests: Aramaic Biblical Targums, Dead Sea Scrolls.

Publications: Articles.

---

1. Statements of the Executive Committee in charge of the Program in Comparative Religion which have been examined by the author include catalogue statements under the heading "Comparative Religion" and various committee reports or statements. (An undated report comes from the period when Dean Ashton was still chairman of the Committee and probably was issued in about 1960. Two reports are dated October 10 and December 17, 1963. Both of these were issued when Professor Henry Veatch of the Department of Philosophy was acting Chairman of the Committee.) All quotations are taken from these statements.

2. Course descriptions taken from *Indiana University Bulletin,* College of Arts and Sciences, 1963-64, and from course outlines and syllabi.

3. During the 1964-65 academic year the salaries of Dr. Bowden and Dr. Hill were being paid for the first time by Indiana University. At the same time, they still had the status of lecturers in the University and the question of professorial status continued to be under discussion.

VII

THE "BIBLE CHAIR" PATTERN AT
THE UNIVERSITY OF TEXAS

History and Rationale

"You shall know the truth and the truth shall make you free." These words, carved in stone over the entrance to the main building and appearing almost as a horizontal buttress to the thirty-story tower which is visible for miles, greet all who enter the campus of the University of Texas at the main gate. It is perhaps of small moment, but one wonders how many of the University's approximately 25,000 students could identify the source of this quotation. Texas to be sure is very much a part of Mencken's "Bible belt" and it is very possible that the number might be higher than in a less pious land. In any case, the opportunity to study the source and context of these words is not conspicuous among the vast array of curricular offerings at the University.

That opportunity is not entirely lacking, however. For well over half a century Texas students have had the option of taking "Bible courses" taught by "religious teachers" in "Bible chairs" maintained adjacent to the campus by various religious denominations. During much of this time relevant courses in Biblical languages and literature have also been offered in the English and Classical Departments. But these latter courses have had no formal relationship to the Bible chair offerings and in recent years they have declined in importance. The course on "The Bible in English and American Literature," offered for many years in the English Department, was dropped in 1961 and has not been offered since. Enrollments have also declined in Biblical languages.

The Bible chair pattern has existed at the University of Texas since 1907. It was set up at a time when religious education was conceived largely in terms of Bible study, and it developed in the context of a Bible-centered religious culture. The Bible chair idea, then, was hit upon as a helpful mechanism with which to bridge the gap between the religious culture and the critically oriented university, and, at the same time, as an acceptable device for offering religious education at a state-supported institution. The University of Texas was but one of many state-supported institutions of higher learning which provided for this pattern, but as a major university it undoubtedly exercised considerable influence by example on other schools in the South and Southwest. The Bible chair pattern continues to be quite common in tax-supported institutions of that region. Religious denominations whose greatest strength is in the South and Southwest, such as the Southern Baptists and the Churches of Christ, maintain regular denominational agencies or mechanisms for the establishment and staffing of Bible chairs and appear to be committed to this approach as the most satisfactory one in state colleges and universities.

The regulations under which Bible courses are offered by Bible chairs and accredited by the University of Texas are still much the same as those developed a half century ago. These regulations are listed in a separate section of the *General Information Catalogue* of the main university. This section reads as follows:

VIII. BIBLE COURSES

Credit toward University degrees is given for certain courses offered by the Association of Religious Teachers, under the following regulations intended to maintain the equivalence of these courses with the courses given in the University:

The plant in which the courses credited are given must (1) be located in Austin, convenient to the University; (2) contain adequate classroom facilities—rooms, seats, blackboard, charts, maps, tables; (3) provide a library of books, dictionaries, and lexicons costing at least $500 as an initial expenditure.

The instructors by whom the courses credited are given must (1) be under the control of some permanent religious organization of recognized standing; (2) possess at least the training demaded of instructors in the University; (3) devote their time primarily to teaching; (4) be approved by the standing committee of the College of Arts and Sciences on Bible courses and by the President, subject to final action by the Board of Regents.

The courses credited must (1) be in the field of historical or literary, but not exegetical or doctrinal, study of the Bible; (2) be thoroughly organized, with syllabi showing the outlines and required readings; (3) be of University grade and on a subject suitable for University instruction; (4) be given in regular classes with meetings at least equal in number, in length of period, and in amount of preparation required, to those of a University course involving the credit asked; (5) include regular tests or examinations corresponding to those of the University for other examinations; (6) be subject to the same regulations and supervision as regular courses given in the University.

The students enrolled in the courses for credit (1) may be credited with no more than twelve semester hours in Bible on any bachelor's degree, (2) are subject to the regulations of the Catalogue on the amount of work which may be carried.[1]

The Bible Chair Pattern Today

Bible courses are currently offered under the above regulations by the following organizations: B'nai B'rith Hillel Bible Chair (Jewish), Church of Christ Bible Chair, Lutheran Bible Chair, Newman Club (Catholic), Townes Bible Chair (Baptist), and United Bible Chair (Episcopal, Christian, Methodist, Presbyterian). All of these chairs are financed by private and denominational funds and the classes are conducted in churches or denominational centers adjacent to the campus. It is particularly significant that titles and descriptions of the courses offered by these chairs appear in no catalogue of the University. Course titles, times and places of meeting, and names of instructors do appear as a separate listing toward the end (not in alphabetical order) of the final listing of courses made available to students for registration purposes. A separate Bible course table is also provided at registration and is manned by members of the Association of Religious Teachers.

During the 1963-64 academic year seven Bible courses—four open to freshmen and three requiring at least sophomore standing—were offered in various sections. These courses were:

1. Life and Teachings of Jesus—offered in eight sections, two each by the United Bible Chair, the Townes Baptist Bible Chair, and the Newman Club Chair, and one each by the Lutheran Bible Chair and the Church of Christ Bible Chair.

2. Life and Letters of Paul—one section by the Lutheran Chair and one section by the Church of Christ Chair.

3. Introduction to the New Testament—two sections by the Townes Baptist Chair, and single sections by the Lutheran Chair, the United Bible Chair, and the Church of Christ Chair.

4. Religion of the Old Testament—one section by the United Chair and one section by the Hillel Chair.

5. Religious Teachings on Marriage and Morals—two sections by the Newman Chair and one section by the Lutheran Chair.

6. Great Ideas of the Bible—one section by the United Chair and one section by the Newman Chair.

7. The Religion of the Pharisees—one section by the Hillel Chair. It should be noted that none of these courses carries upper division credit. Total enrollment in all of these courses in 1963-64 was 545—213 in the first semester and 332 in the second. Enrollments by courses and for selected years are listed in Table VIII. (See also Table IX.)

Of the nine men who taught Bible courses in 1963-64, three devoted full time to this work and the other six had other formal responsibilities in addition to their teaching. Most of these other six were also ministers to students. All nine Bible course teachers were ordained in their respective denominations. Four had professional clerical degrees, five M.A.'s, and one a Ph.D. degree. These men had the status of instructors without vote on the University Faculty. Together they formed the Association of Religious Teachers, a loosely knit body which serves as the mechanism for formal communication between the University—

TABLE VIII

Enrollments in Accredited Courses in Bible:
University of Texas, Bible Chairs*

Course	1959-60 I	1959-60 II	1960-61 I	1960-61 II	1961-62 I	1961-62 II	1962-63 I	1962-63 II	1963-64 I	1963-64 II
Bible 301: Life & teachings of Jesus										
Church of Christ	19	6	4	13	14	5	10	8	5	11
Lutheran	3	8	4	6	2	2	4	2	7	13
Newman	50	43	36	46	30	48	32	20	22	30
Townes	23	44	21	28	27	30	40	34	47	44
United†	65	46	32	61	30	28	37	33	19	22
Bible 302: Life & letters of Paul										
Church of Christ	4	9	6	6	6	11	6	4	7	4
Lutheran	5	4	2	3	3	4	1		2	5
Newman	9	18	12	6				15		8
Townes	23	6	1	3		6				
United	4		12	4	11		4			3
Bible 304: Intro. to N. T.										
Church of Christ		2	5		9		8		5	
Lutheran	3	3	4	4	2	6	3	6		
Newman										
Townes		4		9	12	17	13	31	18	25
United	14	4	4	14		18	11	9	11	15
Bible 305: Religion of O. T.										
Church of Christ				4		6		9		6
Hillel					4	9	12	17	26	44
Lutheran							2			7
Newman										
Townes	7		6		4		10	6		24
United	10	29	21	17	10	12	9	6	6	
Bible 317W: Religious Teachings on Marriage & Morals										
Church of Christ										
Hillel										
Lutheran	5		8	9	10			14	7	22
Newman	32	53	25	59	35	37	38	33	22	46
Townes	6	5	13	6	5	9				
United	40	29								
Bible 318K: Great Ideas of Bible										
Newman									5	
United		9						14	4	1
Bible 319K: Religion of Pharisees								4		2

* Figures supplied by the Association of Religious Teachers. Figures include all initial registrants.

† The "United" figures throughout stand for the combined total of the Wesley Bible Chair, the Presbyterian Bible Chair, and the Texas Bible Chair prior to the Fall of 1961.

TABLE IX

Enrollments in Bible Chairs:*

University of Texas

Bible Chairs	1955-56		1956-57		1957-58		1958-59		1959-60		1960-61		1961-62		1962-63		1963-64	
Year and Semester	I	II	I	II	I	II	I	II	I	II	I	II	I	II	I	II	I	II
Catholic	133		142		114		100		91	114	73	108	65	85	70	68	49	84
Baptist	202		200		65		88		59	59	41	46	48	62	63	71	65	93
Lutheran	24		39		33		15		16	15	18	22	17	12	10	22	16	47
Church of Christ	34		36		37		29		23	17	15	25	29	22	24	21	17	21
Hillel	128	123	79	84	44	23	23	16	20	14	9	15	4	9	12	21	26	46
Disciples of Christ	49		59				15											
Episcopalian									12	22	9	15						
Methodist	203	219	197	156	133	240	136	155	81	75	45	63	51	58	61	62	40	41
Presbyterian	44	35	43	57	52	52	50	15	10	26	15	27						
Total†	817	843†	691†	773†	478	540†	456	461†	312	342	216	306	214	248	240	265	213	332
Annual†	1660†		1464†		1018†		917†		654		522		462		505		545	

(In 1960-61 the Episcopalian and Methodist figures are joined by a brace in the original.)

* Figures supplied by the Association of Religious Teachers, February 20, 1964.

† Figures incomplete for Spring, 1956, Fall, 1956-57, Spring, 1958, and Spring, 1959. Totals for 1955-56, 1956-57, 1957-58, and 1958-59 are estimates supplied by the Association of Religious Teachers.

and specifically the College of Arts and Sciences—and the Bible chairs. This communication may or may not be channeled through the standing faculty committee on Bible courses.

Syllabi used in the various Bible courses appear to be well prepared and, for the most part, to require a fair amount of solid work on the part of the student. Suggested and required readings include a number of the more obvious texts, some of the basic reference works, and a few what might be called "primary sources." All courses require papers as well as examinations. Texts used in some courses do reveal a certain denominational tinge or assume a specific "faith context." On the other hand, the same text is sometimes used by two or three Bible chairs in teaching different sections of the same course. A sampling of texts used in the Life and Teachings of Jesus will illustrate some of these factors: All of the instructors encourage the use of a modern translation of the New Testament; while the Protestants either suggest or require the Revised Standard Version, the Catholic Chair requires the Confraternity Edition. Both the United and the Lutheran Chairs require Bornkamm, *Jesus of Nazareth,* as a text, and the United Chair also requires *Gospel Parallels* edited by Throckmorton and the Hammond *Atlas of the Bible Lands,* while the Lutheran Chair requires Franzmann's *Follow Me* (Concordia). Other texts required by other chairs include: the Newman Catholic Chair—Rochford, *Pattern of Scripture* (Canterbury Press); Heaney, *Faith, Reason and the Gospels* (Newman Press); Sheed, *To Know Christ* (Sheed and Ward); Vawter, "The Bible is Different" (pamphlet, S. A. Guild Press); and two pamphlets in the Paulist Press series entitled Hunt, "The Book of Genesis," and Murphy, "The Book of Exodus"; the Church of Christ Chair—Tenney, *New Testament Survey* (Eerdmans); and the Townes Baptist Chair—Tilden, *Toward Understanding Jesus* (Prentice-Hall) and Stewart, *The Life and Teaching of Jesus Christ* (Abingdon).

Similarities and differences in approach are also evident in the various course descriptions and outlines. Selections from statements of purpose of two courses illustrate this:

Life and Teachings of Jesus

The major objective of the course shall be to recover an accurate and vivid sense of the Jesus of the Synoptic Gospels [United Chair]

* * * * * *

Major objectives. To furnish the student on a freshman level a sound scriptural basis for his understanding of the Christian revelation. [Newman Chair]

(T)o examine the historical context of the life of Jesus in the first century, to study the sources upon which our understanding of Jesus is dependent, and to analyze the mission, message, and results of his ministry as interpreted in the life of the church. [Church of Christ Chair]

*   *   *   *   *   *

(T)o make a thorough investigation of the Biblical source material on the life and teachings of Jesus. [Lutheran Chair]

*   *   *   *   *   *

To point out to the student that every view of life, whether of philosophical, scientific or theological orientation, is a faith commitment based on certain presuppositions. [Townes Baptist Chair]

The Religion of the Old Testament

(T)o show the faith and life situation of the people of the Old Testament and to discern how throughout their history their religious understanding was refined. [Lutheran Chair]

*   *   *   *   *   *

The Old Testament will be approached as the repository of a living tradition, a collection of writings which together bear record to the unique conviction of the people of Israel that their God acts and reveals himself in history. [United Bible Chair]

*   *   *   *   *   *

The Bible will be reviewed from a number of standpoints: traditional Jewish commentators, recent archaeological discoveries, and the historical development of the religion of Irsael. [Hillel Chair]

The three courses that are offered at the sophomore level can be labeled "Bible courses" only if that designation is construed rather broadly. The first of these, Great Ideas of the Bible, deals primarily with major theological concepts of Christianity. In the United Bible Chair course of this title considerable emphasis is put on readings from such contemporary theologians as Barth, Bonhoeffer, Buber, Bultmann, the Niebuhrs, and Tillich, as well as from the Bible itself. The Newman Chair course of this title is concerned primarily with the Catholic tradition. Readings are assigned from the Bible and from such contemporary authors as Danielou, Weigel, Gilson, Heaney, Sheed, Davis, and Sloyan.

The second sophomore course, Religious Teachings on Marriage and Morals, is offered by two chairs, Lutheran and Catholic. The stated objectives of the first of these are "to take an honest look at the situation today in the area of sex, marriage and morals, to trace historically the positions taken and with constant reference to the biblical record lead the class to a realistic view of these areas." The Newman Chair course is "designed to present to the student the traditional Christian positions on the institution of marriage and some basic moral principles derived from the Bible." (Enrollment figures indicate that these are among the more popular of the Bible courses.)

The third of the sophomore courses, The Religion of the Pharisees, was instituted by the Hillel Chair in the Fall of 1963. This course is designed "to reveal the distinctiveness of Pharisaic thinking." Stress is laid on "the relation of the Pharisees to the Bible and their method of interpreting scripture as a means of harmonizing it with changing conditions of life," and an effort is made "to correct the misreading of Pharisaism as a religious formalism" by reviewing the "major themes of Pharisaic belief."

In the six year period from 1955-56 to 1961-62 registrations in all Bible chair courses dropped from 1,660 to 462. In the 1963-64 academic year approximately two per cent of the student body at Texas was enrolled in courses that dealt directly with the Bible. Whether one's value judgment of this fact is good, bad, or indifferent, it is evident that the "Bible course—Bible chair" pattern is not a quantitative success at Texas, and a close look at the pattern might also raise serious questions about its qualitative success.

In view of the character of the Bible chair structure, it is not surprising that there is apparently some suspicion that the Bible courses, or at least some of them, are not up to the academic stature ordinarily expected of university courses, and that, in fact, some of them may even be of a catechetical or sectarian nature. It would take careful and thorough investigation to determine whether such suspicions are well founded. A brief review of the situation leads one to conclude that most of the "religious teachers" or Bible chair instructors are endeavoring to make the best of a rather difficult situation. But the structure itself is conducive to academic irregularities, since it is in a class by itself—not having departmental status and not being directly under the control of either a faculty or a university administrator. There are certain built-in barriers to the advancement of scholarly study; the structure lends itself more to a kind of "sheep-tending" approach than to the encouraging of critical scholarship. Furthermore, because of the denominational ties of the chairs and the quite natural faith orientation that this involves, the approach of the courses tends to be more one of preserving and passing on a heritage or a particular position than that of engaging in critical analyses of sources or genuine search for new knowledge.

In a memorandum submitted to the Governor's Committee on Education Beyond the High School, dated February, 1964, the Association of Religious Teachers maintained that "in our culture it should be our particular concern to preserve and to pass on the treasures past and present of the living Judeo-Christian heritage." One cannot object to an emphasis of this sort, but one might ask whether it goes far enough. Certainly it is not entirely adequate to the mood of the contemporary university with its emphasis on research and the discovery of new knowledge.

One type of "objective evidence" by which to judge the academic caliber of the Bible courses is to be found in a comparison of grades assigned in these courses with grades assigned undergraduates in all courses in the College of Arts and Sciences. Such an analysis reveals that grades assigned in Bible courses tend to be higher than the College average.

Bible courses:[2]

(The figures for averages are given in per cent.)

Fall semester, 1962:

  Total hours registered for, 636; total students assigned letter grades, 212.

A	B	C	D	F
17.1	32.9	39.8	5.6	2.8

Spring semester, 1963:

  Total hours registered for, 702; total students assigned letter grades, 234.

A	B	C	D	F
14.5	39.2	33.3	3.9	.8

Fall semester, 1963:

  Total hours registered for, 603; total students assigned letter grades 201.

A	B	C	D	F
12.4	42.8	40.3	1.5	2.0

College of Arts and Sciences:[3]

1962-63 academic year:

Total hours registered for, 315,344.

A	B	C	D	F
14.3	29.7	31.9	12.2	10.1

While figures are not available for earlier years, the general impression among those familiar with the program seems to be that grades in Bible courses tended to be even higher a decade or two ago and that a sincere effort has been made by some associated with these programs to bring grading more in line with accepted academic standards. In any case, the courses do not now appear to have a general reputation among students for being "easy bets" for high grades.

The Bible chair pattern has encountered difficulties at Texas in recent years—especially in the form of declining enrollments and resistance on the part of University officials to any change in the regulations under which the pattern has existed. The decline in enrollment may be in large part the result of changes within the University and in the character of the student body. Students in the College of Arts and Sciences are now expected to take most of their general requirements in their first two years. This means that most freshmen and sophomores will take at least three required courses each semester, thus reducing the opportunity to choose electives. In addition, most students who enter the University as transfers, and the number of such students is growing significantly, are already well along in an area of specialization and have few opportunities to take elective courses—especially elective courses at the elementary level. Furthermore, Bible courses are not listed as options in specific majors in the College of Arts and Sciences.

As a result, in part, of the decline in enrollment and also because of a desire to employ a well qualified full-time teacher, four Protestant Bible chairs—Methodist, Disciples of Christ, Presbyterian, and Episcopalian—joined forces in 1961 to establish the United Bible Chair. A scholar with theological training and with a Ph.D. in English from Princeton University was appointed to give full time to the work of this chair. But enrollments in United Bible Chair courses have been disappointing. In an effort to break out of the existing pattern, the Board of the United Bible Chair recently created a Foundation for Religious Studies and offered to make funds available to the University for assisting in employing scholars in religion to teach in relevant departments in the University. On the initiative of the Philosophy Department the distinguished philosopher of religion, Charles Hartshorne, was appointed Professor of Philosophy in 1962, and the Foundation for Religious Studies paid one-third of his salary during the 1962-63 and 1963-64 academic years. An offer by the Foundation to pay all or part of the salary of a scholar who would teach courses in Biblical literature in either the English or the Classics Department was recently rejected by the University administration on the grounds "that anyone who teaches a course offered by a regular academic department of the University should be paid by the University rather than from an outside source." And beginning in the Fall of 1964 the University assumed full responsibility for Professor Hartshorne's salary. Thus the efforts of the Foundation for Religious Studies have not met with noticeable success—aside from its part in the appointment of Professor Hartshorne—and it appears that the Foundation might cease to exist. Furthermore, the future of the United Bible Chair seems quite precarious.

While other Bible chairs experienced a decline in enrollment up to 1962, the figures for the Spring, 1964 semester indicate a definite upswing in courses of four of these: Newman Catholic, Townes Baptist, Lutheran, and Hillel. Whereas enrollments in the United Bible Chair courses were at an all time low, enrollments in the Lutheran and Hillel chairs were at an all time high for those chairs. (The Hillel Chair was begun in the Fall of 1961; enrollments grew from four that first semester to forty-six in the Spring of 1964.) Enrollments in the Newman Catholic Chair in the Spring of 1964 were well over 50 per cent of the high in the past ten years and those in the Townes Baptist Chair were higher in the Spring of 1964 than they had been in seven years. Enrollments in the sixth chair, the Church of Christ, remained much the same over the decade from 1954 to 1964. (See Table IX.) These variations between chairs appear to be due in large part to two factors—strength of constituency and personality and approach of instructor. The low enrollments in the United Bible Chair courses, as compared with other chairs and with enrollments in courses offered in the Methodist, Presbyterian, Disciples and Episcopalian chairs previous to 1961, could lead to the conclusion that success of the Bible chair program depends on strong support from a particular denominational group. Decline in enrollment has not been as sharp in those instances where the chair is closely related to a denominational religious program. But denominational tie alone does not account fully for the variations between chairs. The fact that student religious affiliation does not correspond completely with denominational tie of Bible chair—that is, that some non-Lutherans take courses in the Lutheran Bible Chair, etc.—would appear to indicate that other factors, such as ability of instructors to attract students, enter in.

Despite the fact that the other Bible chairs appear to be in a somewhat stronger position, in terms of enrollment, than does the United Bible Chair, there seems to be quite general dissatisfaction with the program on the part of members of the Association of Religious Teachers. No doubt some denominations are more firmly committed to the program than others—and some have more to gain from the program than others. Still, most of the teachers seem to agree that the program leaves much to be desired. This general dissatisfaction has expressed itself in an effort to secure changes in the program. In the most recent such attempt, the Association requested that the following changes be made for the Fall semester of 1964:

(1) course designation changed from Bible to Religion;

(2) courses be listed under Religion in the alphabetical sequence of departments of the College of Arts and Sciences in the "Final Announcement of Courses," with an appropriate explanatory note being included to indicate that Religion does not constitute a department;

(3) certain courses be permitted as upper division electives in Religion (all present Bible courses are lower division), to be offered by the Bible chairs under the following conditions: (a) teaching to be done by full-time instructors with academic training equivalent to what is ordinarily expected within the University; (b) each course to be taught by only one instructor (at present several Bible chairs may offer the same course); and (c) academic supervision of these courses to be provided through a council composed of upper division instructors plus members of the Religious Courses Committee of the Faculty;

(4) present maximum of 12 hours of Bible to be retained, but redistributed with a maximum of six hours in lower division electives in Religion and six hours in upper division electives;

(5) religion to be recognized as a "social science" in the listing of minors under degree requirements of the various departments of the College.

These recommendations were presented to the Dean of the College of Arts and Sciences. He, in turn, submitted them to the Committee on Degrees and Courses. Every recommendation was rejected by that Committee. The Committee recommended instead that the "establishment of advanced courses in religion come only through the initiative of existing departments and be taught within such existing departments," and that "when and if sufficient interest is evidenced in existing departments, the proper avenue of development is an interdepartmental program, and an eventual department (or School, etc.) of religion."[4]

Conclusions

This series of recommendations and counter-recommendations points up sharply the anomalous position in which the Bible chairs exist at the University of Texas. In effect, the Bible chair structure is in a class by itself, being "neither fish nor fowl." The mechanism for handling Bible courses bears little similarity to standard departmental organization. Procedures for handling Bible chair affairs in the University appear to be more of an *ad hoc* than a regularized nature. The College of Arts and Sciences faculty committee on Bible courses appears to operate more in a staff than a line capacity, more as a recommending and advisory than a decision-making group. Bible course teachers have neither professorial rank nor voting power in the faculty. They are, at best, second class citizens in the academic community. Bible courses are neither all the way in nor all the way out of the curricular structure. They can be offered only at the elementary or lower division level and they do not fit integrally into the curriculum of any department or of the College of Arts and Sciences as a whole. In effect, they are appendages, and because of their nature and sponsorship they can become more catechetical than academic in nature. The program, then, is effectively sealed off from normal academic growth and development. Advanced study is an impossibility. By its very nature, the Bible chair pattern tends to inhibit any genuine attempt to treat religion as an integral part of a liberal arts program. It seems, at best, to be a concession to a religious environment and an appendix to the essential task of the University. One University official suggested that the Bible chair pattern is indicative of the University's friendliness toward religion. A person interested in the systematic and scholarly study of religion might, to the contrary, be excused for preferring enmity to this sort of friendship.

The situation is one which might well give rise to a certain amount of soul searching. And, indeed, this seems to have occurred in recent years. As indicated above, efforts have been made to improve the academic caliber of the Bible courses and to develop a more extensive curriculum in religion. But these efforts have been confined largely to those directly responsible for the Bible chair program. While the Bible chair pattern and the status of Bible courses have also been topics of formal and informal discussions within the University, such discussions appear to have borne little fruit. The *status quo* has been maintained. In fact, one has the impression that University discussion about the validity and future of the Bible chair pattern, and even about the more general and basic question of the scholarly study of religion, has been at dead center. No source of movement or direction has been visible.

Whether the existence of such an anomalous structure as the Bible chair pattern has actually worked to the disadvantage of the systematic, scholarly study of religion at Texas is not entirely clear. It is clear, however, that significant advancement of such study will require either a radical revision or a complete abandonment of the Bible chair pattern along with systematic cultivation of the academic field of religion. This is not to say that the scholarly study of religion does not take place at Texas. But what teaching is done in this area—aside from the Bible chairs—occurs more or less incidentally in such existing departments as Anthropology, English, Classics, History, and Philosophy. (Relevant courses in these departments, together with enrollments for recent years, are listed in Table X.) A clearly designated formal structure for the systematic encouragement of the study of religion could encourage the addition of other relevant courses and perhaps even develop a co-ordinated curriculum in this area.

The most significant recent development relating to the study of religion at the University of Texas is the appointment of Professor Charles Hartshorne to the Philosophy Department. Acknowledged to be one of America's major philosophers of religion, he has had a distinguished career of teaching and writing. He was recently designated as one of a number of "Ashbel Smith Professors" in the University of Texas. These professorships, which exist in several departments, are granted to exceptionally distinguished scholars on the faculty of the University. The appointment of a man of the stature and interests of Professor Hartshorne bodes well for the scholarly study of religion at Texas; it encourages a hopeful conclusion to this otherwise quite critical account.

TABLE X

Enrollments in Selected Courses Related to Religion:
University of Texas*

Course	1956-57 I	II	1958-59 I	II	1960-61 I	II	1961-62 I	II	1962-63 I	II	1963-64 I	II
Anthropology 364. Magic, Witchcraft, and Religion			37		38		76	184				
Classics 619. Elementary New Testament Greek ..	31	31	33	33	27	27			11	11	6	6
Classics 628. New Testament Greek ..	6	6	9	9	3	3	11	11	10	10		
Classics 684. Studies in Biblical Literature†												
English 358K. Bible in English & American Literature			18		16							
History 343. Age of Reformation					21		27		24			56
History 362K. Medieval Civilization	34			54	21		37				68	
History 364N. Medieval Islam									6‡			
Philosophy 301. Intro. Philosophical Inquiries			75	124	116	272	126	274	194	382	308	396
Philosophy 356. Philosophy of Religion	63		65	50	60	93		98	65	90	42	
Philosophy 368K. Idea of God in Great Philosophical Systems ..									61		20	
Philosophy 379. Conflict Between Faith and Reason†												

* Figures supplied by the office of the Dean, College of Arts and Sciences.
† Listed but not offered in years selected.
‡ Taught by a visiting professor.

*Biographical Information, Association of Religious Teachers:
University of Texas—1964*

REV. CHARLES H. BORN, *Lutheran Bible Chair*

Age 33. Concordia Seminary, St. Louis, Mo., B.A. 1946, Diploma of
Vocation, B.D. 1949; Marquette University, Milwaukee, Wisc.,
1949-50, graduate work in history.

Teaching Experience: Concordia, Seward, Nebr., 1954-55.

REV. CHARLES H. COX, JR., *United Bible Chair*

Age 33. Birmingham Southern College, B.A. 1951; Yale Divinity School, B.D. 1955; Ph.D. residence requirements completed, Vanderbilt University.

REV. DONALD R. FLETCHER, *United Bible Chair*

Age 45. Princeton University, A.B. 1939; Princeton Theological Seminary B.D., 1943; Princeton University, Ph.D. (English) 1951.

Teaching Experience: Teaching Bible at University of Texas with Presbyterian Bible Chair, 1960-61; United Bible Chair, 1961-.

REV. BILL B. GLOVER, *Townes Baptist Bible Chair*

Age 34. University of New Mexico, 1948-51; Baylor University, B.A. 1954; Southwestern Baptist Theological Seminary, B.D. 1957; Baylor University, M.A. 1958; residence requirements completed, Th.D., Southwestern Baptist Theological Seminary.

Teaching Experience: Arlington State College (Bible teacher), 1960-62.

REV. GUSTAV KOPKA, JR., *Lutheran Bible Chair*

Age 31. Concordia College, Moorhead, Minn., B.A. 1954; Diploma, Luther Theological Seminary, St. Paul, Minn., 1958; Creighton University, Omaha, Nebr., M.A. 1957; graduate study, State University of Iowa, Iowa City, Iowa, 1959-60.

RABBI SHELDON LILKER, *Hillel B'nai B'rith Bible Chair*

Age 32. Queens College, B.A.; Hebrew Union College, Jewish Institute of Religion (New York), M.A.; graduate student, Hebrew University in Jerusalem.

REV. WILLIAM F. MCAULIFFE, *Newman Catholic Bible Chair*

Age 35, College of the Holy Cross, Worcester, A.B. 1951; Harvard, Business School, 1954-55; St. Paul's College, Washington, D.C., M.A. 1961.

Teaching Experience: Catholic Information Center, Toronto, 1960; Catholic Information Center, Boston, 1961-62.

REV. DAVID O'BRIEN, *Newman Catholic Bible Chair*

Age 35. St. Bonaventure University, Olean, New York, B.A. 1950; The Catholic University of Washington, D. C. (St. Paul's College), M.A. 1955.

H. GENE PATTERSON, *Church of Christ Bible Chair*

Age 33. Abilene Christian College, B.A. 1952; Harding College, Searcy, Ark, M.A. 1957.

Teaching Experience: Instructor, Cabot, Arkansas, School System, 1953; Assistant Professor of Greek and Bible, York College, York, Nebr., 1955-59.

---

1. 1963-64 issue, p. 109.

2. Figures for Bible courses furnished by the Association of Religious Teachers. Discrepancies between these figures and those found in Tables VIII and IX are due to the fact that the figures given in the Tables include all initial registrants whereas these include only those assigned grades for credit.

3. *Report of the Registrar*, 1962-63, The University of Texas (December 1, 1963), Table 6.

4. Memorandum to the College of Arts and Sciences from the Association of Religious Teachers regarding changes in course designation and course listings, February 26, 1964. Memorandum to the Association of Religious Teachers from the Dean of the College of Arts and Sciences regarding the action of the Committee on Degrees and Courses, March 16, 1964.

VIII

A CURRICULUM IN RELIGIOUS STUDIES UNDER SPECIAL PROGRAMS IN HUMANITIES

Stanford University

History and Rationale

Stanford University has developed an imaginative and productive curriculum in religious studies which is indigenous to the context of the humanities. This curriculum is a special program in the humanities, in the School of Humanities and Sciences, and under the direction of a committee chaired by the executive head of Humanities (Special Programs) and made up of the men who offer courses in the curriculum and of other selected faculty. Instituted in its present administrative form in 1951, the curriculum in religious studies has been a thriving enterprise ever since and gives every evidence of further growth and continuing vitality. In a significant measure this success has been due to the fact that the study of religion has been approached as integral to the humanities. This has had the double effect of relating the study of religion to the strong humanities emphasis which has been characteristic of Stanford and of forestalling an isolation of religion—either as an area of specialization of interest to a limited number of students or as a subject taught primarily for edification and moral uplift. A careful effort has been made to offer course work in religion that is both scholarly and relevant to student interest and the context of inquiry within the humanities, and under a faculty of able teaching scholars who have special competence in some aspect of religious studies and are committeed to relating religious studies to fundamental issues of human life and culture.

Stanford University was founded in the late nineteenth century under a charter which included a prohibition against "sectarian instruction," but called for the teaching of "the immortality of the soul, the existence of an all-wise and benevolent Creator, and that obedience to His laws is the highest duty of man." The founders and benefactors of the University, Senator and Mrs. Leland Stanford, directed the building of a Memorial Church at the very center of the campus, with the understanding that this edifice would be a symbol and instrument of the sentiments expressed in the charter. They also provided for the employment of a chaplain, hoping to find a man who would be "strong enough and broad enough to fill the demands of any creed, all creeds or no creed . . . a simple follower of Christ."[1]

The sentiments of the founders, which were sentiments typical of a kind of generalized American Protestantism, may have found expression to a degree in a building and in "non-sectarian" religious services and activities, but little effort was made to give them formal embodiment in the curriculum of the developing university. From time to time the chaplain offered courses in such areas as Bible and Philosophy of Religion, and a course on "The Bible as Literature" became a standard offering of the Department of English. But it was not until 1951 that a well organized curriculum in religious studies was developed under a formal structure. From its beginnings this curriculum was disassociated from any formal tie with the Memorial Church or any sort of religious activities. Significantly, religion was accepted as an area of academic study within the humanities. While it was not inconceivable that the study of religion could concern itself with the type of sentiments expressed by the founders or could have implications for the religious life, the approach and context of this study were to be academic in nature and devoted primarily to intellectual inquiry, not catechetical indoctrination or moral formation.

In 1951 Alexander Miller, specialist in Christian thought and Christian ethics, was appointed Lecturer in Religion, and began what was to become a distinguished and influential career at Stanford. During the years Professor Miller spent there (1951 until his death in 1960) the curriculum in religious studies grew and a carefully conceived rationale was worked out—under the leadership of Professor Miller and with the assistance of the committee in charge of the curriculum. An early indication of the direction of the rationale developed by Mr. Miller is evident in the contrast between the statement on religion in the 1950-51 "Announcement of Courses" and its counterpart for 1951-52:

> The study of religion is conducted in the spirit of objective inquiry. Inasmuch as Stanford University is undenominational, the courses in religion are impartial in regard to sectarian differences. The instruction is designed to aid the general student in the double task of understanding the roots of our civilization and developing his personal attitude toward the Ultimate. (1950-51)

*   *   *   *   *

> The purpose of the program is to introduce students to the world-view of Biblical Religion as it has been developed and interpreted in the Western tradition and has been related to Western society. The study is systematic, historical, and

comparative, with a double intention: to enable students critically to appraise the religious traditions in which they stand, and to supply them with the intellectual basis for a personal judgment. (1951-52)

The main course which had been offered before 1951-52 was Comparative Religion taught by a specialist in Indian studies. It was described as an analysis of "the leading conceptions of the great world religions: Hinduism, Buddhism, Taoism, Confucianism, Shinto, Zoroastrianism, Manicheism, and Mohammedanism," and involving a comparison of these conceptions with "the leading ideas of Christianity." This course continued after 1951 as a standard offering in religious studies. Most of the other courses which constituted the new curriculum were instituted by Miller. A sample listing of these courses gives a further indication of the nature of his interest and of the developing rationale of the program:[2]

Biblical Literature and Religion
History of Christian Social Thought
Christianity and Contemporary Social Systems
Contemporary Movements in Christian Thought
The Christian View of Man and the World
Christian Ethics—Christian Political Thought

The Christian Faith and University Education, which was instituted as a lower division course in 1953, indicates Miller's concern that the study of religion be related to the total university enterprise and to the life of the students. This course was described as "an introductory course in the Christian faith and its relation to the life of the university." Topics considered were "the character of a university," "the vocation of a student," "the nature and ground of Christian faith and its relation to the main university concerns," and "contemporary issues in the area of faith and knowledge." Professor Miller considered this course a point of entry into other work in the program although not a prerequisite to other courses.

Professor Miller was convinced of the centrality to the curriculum of courses such as Christian Political Thought and Christianity and Contemporary Society. These represented efforts to relate Christianity to aspects of Western culture and to deal with topics and issues of relevance to such academic areas as political science. Dr. Miller felt that the curriculum in religious studies should constantly seek to relate itself to the underlying assumptions and "presuppositions" of such academic disciplines as political science, history and philosophy. This conviction sprang in large part from his own conception of the nature of religion, Christianity, and Christian theology. He stressed Professor Paul Tillich's view that "religion is the substance of culture, and culture is the expression of religion." Given this broad definition, one could not do justice to religion by treating it as but one segment of human life and culture. Religion, as a *dimension* rather than an *area* of life, has implications for all human endeavors and, in effect, for all academic disciplines. Thus Miller opposed the establishment of a separate department of religion, staffed by specialists who would apply their own methodologies to a specific, carefully defined and limited area of human life and culture. Since religion and culture are so intimately related, the study of religion calls for specialists (actually theologians) who can relate their work to that of scholars in other intellectual disciplines. The structure in which such men work should be "comprehensive and *not* departmental." Thus it was regarded as being entirely logical that the curriculum in religious studies should be one of the special progams in humanities.[3]

Miller and his colleagues sought to persuade specific departments "to establish work of a *frontier* kind." Thus the two quarters in Christian Political Thought (which was "in effect the historical and systematic theology of politics") came to be listed as an elective for majors in political science. To this end also, work in religious studies came to be accepted as a minor for students majoring in English and in history. In part as a result of Professor Miller's encouragement, courses on subjects touching religion or of religious significance were also instituted in other departments, taught not by faculty members of the curriculum in religious studies but by members of the departments concerned.

Professor Miller actually preferred the use of the word "theology" to "religion" to designate what he had in mind. He maintained that theology is an intellectual discipline which has a legitimate place in the academic community. He argued, further, that theology is the articulate and systematic expression of a community of faith, and that it maintains its vitality only as it continues to be related in some way to that community. The theologian, then, is one who stands "within the theological circle" (Tillich's phrase), who shares "the faith of the community." In response to the contention that this would represent a denial of the university's standard of objectivity, Miller argued that objectivity in the sense of "detachment from or suspension from all conviction" is "both illusory and, from the point of view of fruitful academic work, undesirable." If objectivity, on the other hand, can be interpreted to mean "scholarly fairness," this can be "authentically secured not by the disinfection of the university against conviction, but by the clash and conflict of a variety of convictions." Miller recognized that such a position raised another question stemming from the fact that there is no single prevailing community of faith in our culture. In response to this fact of American life he suggested that not only Protestant theologians but also Jewish and Roman Catholic theologians should be involved in the academic enterprise. And he argued further that his position in this regard was more in keeping with the Stanford charter, as well as reality, than the notion of some sort of a "neutral intellectual religion unrelated to the conviction of communities . . . ."[4]

Miller's position is worth considering at some length because of its inherent interest and its influence on the development of the curriculum in religious studies. Aspects of this position continue to be evident in the rationale of the present curriculum and the projections of the faculty committee in charge.

Faculty, Curriculum and Plans for Development
1963-64

In 1963-64 there were three faculty members teaching full time in the curriculum in religious studies. Their areas of specialization were Biblical studies and Hebrew, history of Christian thought, and contemporary religious thought. The enrollments in courses taught by these men have increased substantially in recent years (387 in 1960-61, 449 in 1961-62, 814 in 1962-63 and 733 in 1963-64. For details, see Table XI.) The most recent plans of the committee in charge call for the possible addition of three more scholars—one in Jewish studies, one in Roman Catholic studies, and one in non-Western religions. As a result of increasing enrollments and expanding course offerings it is possible that for reasons of greater administrative efficiency the curriculum might develop into a department. While such a development might also involve the institution of a major—and possibly even graduate work—it appears that a continuing effort will be made to relate studies in religion to the context of the humanities.

Robert McAfee Brown was appointed in 1962 to succeed the late Alexander Miller. Professor Brown, who had been Auburn Professor of Systematic Theology at Union Theological Seminary, New York, from 1953 until 1962, is a Protestant theologian who is committed to

TABLE XI

Enrollments in Selected Courses in Religion:
Stanford University*

Course	1956-57	1958-59	1960-61	1961-62	1962-63	1963-64
R100. Comparative Religion	260	122	132	209		
R101. Ancient Cultures of Near East	7	14	11			
R102. Old Testament	30	51	59	50	59	43
R103. New Testament	35	31	50	42	33	42
R104. History of Christian Thought: to A.D. 1500			9	19	33	55
R105. History of Christian Thought: since A.D. 1500			5	27	21	52
R106. Protestant Reformation			6	8	14	29
R110. Christian Political Thought: Historical	14	22				
R111. Christian Political Thought: Contemporary	17	37				
R112. Christianity and Contemporary Society	58	47				
R113. Intro. Christian Thought	50	25	5			
R114. Christian Ethics	49	37	19	29	108	100
R115. Contemporary Trends in Religious Thought					128	
R120. Religion in America			5		21	25
R150. Christian Classics	19	24	48	33	79	
R155. Prophets of Israel	8	10		5		
R160. Myth and Wisdom in Israel		7				15
R165. Four Gospels	12	15	13		4	
R170. Paul and Early Church				5		8
R182. Theology and Contemporary Literature					266	327
R186. Theology of History				10	11	19
R187. Christian Thought in 19th Century				2	5	
R190. Christianity and Culture	24	18	12	10	15	
R199. Individual Work	4	14	13		17	18
Totals: Curriculum in Religious Studies	587	474	387	449	814	733
History 110. Age of Reformation	117	109		45	126	121
History 111. Humanism, Protestantism, and Catholicism					89	
History 318. Course of Christian Humanism				15	18	15

(Continued on Next Page)

Table XI (*Continued*)

Course	1956-57	1958-59	1960-61	1961-62	1962-63	1963-64
Philosophy 101. Early Christian, Medieval, and Renaissance Philosophy	35	40	25	21	25	19
Philosophy 180. Philosophy of Religion	14				33	
Classics HE 1, 2, 3. 1st-yr. Hebrew			12	9	9 (1 & 2 only)	12
Classics HE 22, 23. 2nd-yr. Hebrew				2	3	1
Classics HE 101. 3rd-yr. Hebrew				1		
English 100. English Bible as Literature			16	18	15	13

* All of these are one-term courses. (Figures for Hebrew 1, 2, 3, and 22, 23 are for three quarters and two quarters, respectively.) Figures supplied by the office of the Director, Special Programs in Humanities.

relating the theological enterprise to contemporary social and existential issues. (His most popular course at Stanford has been Theology and Contemporary Literature.) He has also participated actively in an inter-religious dialogue involving Catholics and Protestants. He is the co-author, with the late Gustave Weigel, S.J., of *An American Dialogue;* he was one of the official non-Catholic observers at the second session of the Second Vatican Council (see his *Observer in Rome*); and he has written a regular column for the lay Catholic journal, *Commonweal*. Professor Brown's commitment to theology and his interest in inter-religious relations and discussions has led him to play an active role in shaping the plan to appoint scholars in Jewish and Roman Catholic studies. It appears that under Dr. Brown's influence the vigorous theological exchange involving men of various views—which Miller had urged—will become a reality at Stanford. A major step was taken in this direction with the appointment of the Reverend Daniel J. O'Hanlon, S.J., as Visiting Professor of Religion for the academic year 1964-65. It is hoped that during this interval a permanent appointment can be made in the area of Roman Catholic studies.

Courses currently listed in the curriculum in religious studies include:

The Ancient Cultures of the Near East
Old Testament
New Testament
History of Christian Thought
The Protestant Reformation
Introduction to Christian Thought
Christian Ethics
Christianity and Culture
Contemporary Trends in Religious Thought
Religion in America
Christian Classics
The Prophets of Israel
Myth and Wisdom in Israel
The Four Gospels
Paul and the Early Church
Theology and Contemporary Literature
Theology of History
Christian Thought in the Nineteenth Century
Individual Work

Nearly all of these are one-quarter, four-unit courses offered without prerequisite. There is no suggested sequence of courses. Comparative Religion, formerly a standard course, has not been offered since the retirement in 1962 of the professor who had taught it.

Courses in the Biblical area have been taught by Professor Edwin Good. Following is a description of the approach, content, and requirements of two of these courses which were offered during the 1963-64 academic year:[5]

Old Testament.

The nature of the Hebrew religion; prophet and priest; history of the Messianic idea; the Old Testament in Judaism and Christianity. Subjects discussed included: the chosen people, the ethical dimension, expectation and reality, worship and wisdom, and much emphasis was placed upon specific and relevant passages in the Old Testament. In addition to a final examination, students were required to write a brief essay on a relevant topic of their own choosing which included careful examination of some part of the text of the Old Testament.

Required readings: assignments from the Revised Standard Version of the Old Testament and Napier, *Song of the Vineyard.*

Recommended readings included Eichrodt, *Man in the Old Testament;* Good, *You Shall be my People;* Szikszai, *The Story of Israel;* and Wright, *The Old Testament Against Its Environment.*

New Testament.

Relation of Christianity to Judaism and to the Hellenistic world; Gospels as documents of faith; faith and theology of Paul.

Topics discussed included: the critical method, some current issues in New Testament study including cultural contexts of the New Testament, the historical Jesus, demythologization, Gnosticism and the New Testament period, and such principal themes as the character of faith, the future of faith, the imperative of faith, and the community of faith.

Required readings: Revised Standard Version of the New Testament, and Crownfield, *A Historical Approach to the New Testament.* Recommended readings included Bultmann, *Primitive Christianity* and *Jesus and the Word;* Toombs, *the Threshold of Christianity;* and Beker, *The Church Faces the World.*

Of the courses offered by Professor Brown, I have chosen to describe four:

Introduction to Christian Thought.

Systematic presentation of the content of the Christian faith. Treatment is "topical rather than historical," but historical material is used to illustrate how a given conviction has developed. Topics discussed included: theology as a discipline; revelation—"the key issue"; and the doctrines of God, man, Christ, the church and the sacraments, and eschatology.

The approach is basically Protestant with some comparison of Protestant and Catholic convictions in given areas.

Texts: Horton, *Christian Theology: An Ecumenical Approach* and Whale, *Christian Doctrine.* Also used: Williams, *What Present-Day Theologians Are Thinking* and Forell, *The Protestant Faith.* Relevant sections assigned in *A Handbook of Christian Theology,* Cohen, ed., and a list of more "advanced" books which might be called sources.

Christian Ethics.

Discussion of both historical and contemporary issues. The latter include: race, work and vocation, war, sex and marriage, and political responsibility.

Readings—Beach & Niebuhr, eds., *Christian Ethics* is the text for the historical section. Selected readings include Brunner, *The Divine Imperative.*

Religion in America.

Major religious forces at work in America today and analysis of Protestantism, Roman Catholicism and Judaism—total ethos of the three faiths and survey of ways in which the three groups are seeking to relate to each other.

Readings required: Herberg, *Protestant—Catholic—Jew;* Hudson, *American Protestantism;* Ellis, *American Catholicism;* Glazer, *American Judaism;* Adam, *The Spirit of Catholicism;* Brown, *The Spirit of Protestantism;* Steinberg; *Basic Judaism;* and Brown and Weigel, *An American Dialogue.* Selected portions from Berger, *The Noise of Solemn Assemblies* or Marty, *The New Shape of American Religion;* and *Religion in America,* Cogley, ed.; *The Shaping of American Religion,* Smith and Jamison, eds.; Dillenberger and Welch, *Protestant Christianity.* Term paper required.

Theology and Contemporary Literature.

Religious and theological convictions as expressed, both overtly and covertly, in certain contemporary writers. Books have been chosen not primarily by the test of literary excellence or religious orthodoxy, but for the sensitivity with which they deal with "the enduring aspects of Man's situation" and the manner in which they raise questions, "from whatever perspective" with which "religion and theology must grapple."

Reading required. One book in order to become acquainted with some of the content of the Christian faith (many students have had no previous course in religion): Whale, *Christian Doctrine* or (less difficult) Forell, *The Protestant Faith;* and Adam, *The Spirit of Catholicism,* for Roman Catholics. Topics and books in the course: (1) The present as a time of waiting— Beckett, *Waiting for Godot* and Auden, *For the Time Being;* (2) dimensions of man's predicament—Miller, *The Death of a Salesman,* Golding, *Lord of the Flies,* Camus, *The Fall,* and Agee, *A Death in the Family;* (3) dimensions of redemption: a theme with many variations—a. faith in man (Salinger, *The Catcher in the Rye,* Steinbeck, *East of Eden* and Warren, *All the King's*

Men)—b. shadows of grace (Eliot, *The Family Reunion,* Sayers, *The Zeal of Thy House,* Silone, *Bread and Wine,* Green, *The Power and the Glory,* and Paton, *Cry, The Beloved Country.*)

Courses have regularly been offered in the history of Christian thought. Through the Spring of 1964 Professor Forstman had taught these courses—offering a two-quarter sequence in the development of Christian thought, one quarter dealing with the period to 1500 and the other with the modern period and especially with Protestantism, and a third quarter dealing with the theology of the Protestant Reformation. With a change of faculty personnel in this area—Professor Forstman moved to another institution and was replaced in the Fall of 1964 by Professor Clebsch—a full-year sequence was projected in the history of Christian thought.

A number of courses of relevance to the study of religion are listed as part of the curricular offerings of the standard academic areas at Stanford. A sampling from the latest catalogue reveals the following among these: Anthropological Approaches to Religion and Philosophy, with an emphasis on anthropological theories relating to the origin and nature of religion taught by Professor Beals in Anthropology; courses in New Testament Greek and in Hebrew in Classics; The English Bible as Literature, taught by Professor Ford in English with an emphasis on readings in Old Testament, New Testament and selected books of the Apocrypha, and "with some attention to history of the English Bible and use made of Biblical themes in English literature"; various courses of relevance in History, including those in Ancient, Medieval and early modern history, and specifically, Age of the Reformation, and Humanism, Protestantism and Catholicism, taught by Professor Spitz; Philosophy of Religion, in Philosophy; and Religious Institutions and Behavior, taught by Professor Dornbusch in Sociology.

Under the General Studies Program at Stanford, two Senior Colloquia are required of all seniors who are candidates for the A.B. degree, with a few exceptions. These Senior Colloquia are limited to fifteen students each and "are built around subjects or issues of continuing importance, or basic documents of enduring significance. They are designed to stimulate serious thought rather than to impart information for its own sake. Thus the emphasis is on discussion and analysis, not lectures."[6] For the most part students are not permitted to take Senior Colloquia in their own areas of specialization.

Senior Colloquia are offered on a wide variety of topics. To an extent, the Senior Colloquium is regarded by faculty members as an opportunity to explore with a small number of students a subject of interest and excitement to the faculty member as well as of relevance to student interest. Generally these are two quarter-unit courses. Colloquia of relevance to the field of religion, among those listed in the 1963-64 catalogue, include: The Thought of Reinhold Niebuhr, taught by Professor Brown; Theology and Literary Criticism (study of such writers as St. Augustine, Luther, Pascal, Mathew Arnold, and T. S. Eliot), taught by Professor Hyde of Modern European Languages; Faith and Freedom: The Thought of Rudolf Bultmann, taught by Professor Forstman; The End of All Things (a "discussion of various theories of the goal and end of history or what is technically known as Eschatology," with special attention to "classical, Christian, liberal, reactionary and Marxist theories and to the 'end of the world' problem at the present time"), taught by Professor Otis of Classics; Ceremony and Symbol in Religion and Society, taught by Chaplain Minto; Modern Islam and Islamic Nationalism, taught by Professor C. Harris of Political Science; and Mystics and Mysticism, taught by Professor Watkins of Political Science.

Conclusions

Within a period of little more than a decade Stanford has developed an exciting and quite substantial curriculum in religious studies as a special program in Humanities. The Stanford undergraduate has ample opportunity to study aspects of the Western religious heritage and the relation between religion and contemporary social, cultural and existential issues under a stimulating faculty which is made up of a core of teachers in religious studies and includes a number of professors in more established disciplinary areas. To date the curriculum in religious studies has been designed entirely for the general or liberal arts education of undergraduates. As such, it is a success both quantitatively and qualitatively. Whether specialization at the undergraduate and graduate levels is desirable, and how this might affect the present program if attempted, remains to be seen.

The Stanford Curriculum as presently constituted is heavily weighted toward the West and specifically toward Protestant Christianity. Thus the addition to the faculty of permanent appointments in Jewish and Roman Catholic studies would provide a measure of balance, as would the introduction or re-introduction of substantial work in non-Western religions.

Program in Religious Studies: Stanford University;
Faculty, 1963-64

ROBERT MCAFEE BROWN, *Professor*
B. 1920. Amherst College, B.A.; Union Theological Seminary, B.D.;
Columbia University, Ph.D.; studied at Mansfield College, Ox-
ford, St. Mary's College, St. Andrews University, Scotland.
Publications: P. T. Forsyth: Prophet for Today, 1952; *The Bible
Speaks to You,* 1955; *The Significance of the Church,* 1956; *An
American Dialogue,* with Gustave Weigel, S.J., 1960; *The Spirit
of Protestantism,* 1961; *Observer in Rome,* 1964; translator of
deDietrich, *God's Unfolding Purpose* and Casalis, *Portrait of Karl
Barth.* General editor, Layman's Theological Library (Westminster 12 Volumes); editorial boards: *Christianity and Crisis; Presbyterian Life.*

H. JACKSON FORSTMAN, *Assistant Professor*
B. 1929. Phillips University, B.A.; Union Theological Seminary,
B.D., Th.D.
*Publication: Word and Spirit: Calvin's Doctrine of Biblical Author-
ity,* 1962; contributor to *Encounter, The Pulpit, The Christian.*

EDWIN MARSHALL GOOD, *Associate Professor of Religion and Hebrew*
B. 1928. Westminster College, B.A.; Union Theological Seminary,
B.D.; Columbia University, Ph.D.
Publications: You Shall Be My People: Books of Covenant and Law,
1959. Contributor to *Union Seminary Quarterly Review, Vetus
Testamentum, Journal of Biblical Literature, Journal of General
Education, Interpreter's Dictionary of the Bible.* General Editor,
The Westminster Guides to the Bible.

Faculty, 1964-65

DRS. BROWN and GOOD

WILLIAM A. CLEBSCH, *Associate Professor*
B. 1923. The University of Tennessee, B.A.; Theological Seminary
in Virginia, B.D.; Union Theological Seminary, Th.D.
*Publications: Contemporary Perspectives on Word, World, and
Sacrament* (National Lutheran Council); *England's Earliest
Protestants,* 1964; and *Journals of the Protestant Episcopal
Church in the Confederate States of America,* 1962, ed. Author of
numerous scholarly articles. *Episcopal Overseas Mission Review,*
1955-59, ed.; *Encyclopedia Britannica* and *Twentieth Century En-
cyclopedia of Religious Knowledge,* contributor.

DANIEL J. O'HANLON, S.J., *Visiting Professor*
Co-author, with Hans Küng and Yves Congar, *The Council Speeches of Vatican II. Christianity Divided,* 1964, co-ed. Author of numerous scholarly articles and contributor to popular religious journals.
Permanent position: Professor of Fundamental Theology, Alma College.

---

1. Alexander Miller, *Faith and Learning* (New York, Association Press, 1960), p. 123.

2. Course titles and descriptions taken from various catalogue publications of Stanford University, 1950-1964.

3. For a full discussion of Miller's position, see his *Faith and Learning,* esp. chap. V.

4. *Ibid.,* pp. 136-138.

5. Course descriptions taken from course outlines and syllabi.

6. *Stanford University Bulletin, Courses and Degrees,* 1963-64, p. 456.

IX

A FULL-SCALE DEPARTMENT OF RELIGION OFFERING BOTH UNDERGRADUATE AND GRADUATE SPECIALIZATION

Princeton University

History, Rationale, and Curriculum

The Department of Religion at Princeton, one of the most substantial and flourishing departments in the country, has been in existence for less than twenty years. Since 1946 when Princeton's Program of Religious Studies became a Department, granting a major for the A.B. degree, a rich fare of curricular offerings has been developed and this has proved to be popular among Princeton undergraduates. Since 1955 the Department has also developed a full graduate program which is preparing an increasing number of scholars in various areas of religion. The whole program at Princeton is such that it should be of special interest to any major university contemplating either the establishment of a department of religion or an expansion of an already existing curricular program.

The Department owes its beginnings and basic rationale in no small degree to the work and report of the Special Committee of the Faculty on Religious Education, a committee of six which was appointed by the President in the early 1930's and which issued its Report in 1935. The printed Report of this Committee begins by drawing a clear distinction between "the study of religion and the practice of it," observing that it was a mixture of the two "which bred a suspicion that has in the end driven the study from an independent place in the curriculum . . . ." The Report calls for the restoration of that study to an independent place in the curriculum, a place independent both of religious activities or the chapel and of other academic fields or disciplines. The Committee argues for a place of independence within the academic enterprise on the primary ground that religion "is an independent power . . ." and that "the religious forces in history are distinct with their own essence, development, and effects. Consequently the study of them is a study in itself and not a by-product of the study of other phenomena." Religion "is not literature, not art, not philosophy, however closely it may be related to these other humanities in the life of man."

Granted the independent nature of religion, how will it be studied? The Committee argues for the primacy of the historical approach, the primary method used in the study of the so-called humanities, and suggests further that the initial subject of study should be Christianity, which is, and has been, "without dispute," "the central religious force in the culture of which we are a product . . . ." Achieving "an understanding of what Christianity is . . ." requires a knowledge of the Hebrew religious tradition out of which it grew. Thus the Report recommends as a starting point the institution of two courses at the junior level: (1) The Development of the Religious Thought of the Hebrews, and (2) Religious Thought in the Gospels. To underline its emphasis upon the independent nature of religion and the consequent necessity of a direct and concentrated approach to the subject, the Committee asserts that the first of these courses "should not be primarily about the Old Testament but rather should be centered in what the Old Testament is about."

Reiterating the primacy of the historical approach, the Report indicates, however, that the object "is not to exhibit a mere chronology of history as such, but by means of the chronological sequence and by comparative analysis to show what the religious forces are . . . ." Thus "as the student gradually acquires some knowledge of what is meant by religion, he will naturally and properly wish to consider its nature and value more critically." This suggests a second approach based on but not the same as the historical approach, that is, it calls for a critical and systematic handling of the issues. And, in fact, this approach did come to occupy a central place in the program that got under way some five years following the issuance of the Report.

The Report closes with a brief discussion regarding other possible approaches to the study of religion, and also includes some remarks about the problems of staff and administration. In regard to approaches other than the historical, the Report does recognize the possibility of the "comparative approach," and acknowledges the obvious value of understanding other religions as well as those religions which have been most influential in the West. However, the Report suggests that "no comparative study of religions should be attempted until one religion has been thoroughly mastered." Having pointed out (earlier in the Report) "the sterile nature of starting the study of religion at the anthropological level" the Committee recognizes that "once a genuine insight into the essence of religion in its more developed form has been attained, a knowledge of its primitive beginnings is illuminating, indeed essential, to an adequate understanding of religion as a continuing vital phenomenon." In discussing the psychological and philosophical approaches the Committee suggests that

> as part of the more critical approach to the study of religion, courses on certain aspects of religion such as religious mysticism, religious institutions, the literary and artistic expressions of religion and the relation of religion to the social order and institutions, might eventually be offered if the need arose.

In its discussion of staff and administration, the Report recommends the appointment of a scholar in the history of religion, for whom religion is a primary interest and not "a side issue to another field." Furthermore, this scholar should not "be attached to any existing department," the Report maintains, for "to do so would be to place him and his subject and the department to which he is attached at a singular disadvantage. Departmental policies and work ought not to be distorted to take care of the extraneous element," the Report points out, and, in addition, "the newcomer would hardly be in a position to force recognition of his needs among so many devoted to a different study." At the same time, "it is equally clear," the Report asserts, "that the man in charge of religious courses cannot float at large, administratively speaking, in a university organized by departments." Thus the Report recommends the formation of a faculty "Committee on the Study of Religion" which "should function in lieu of a department . . . ." Finally, the Committee indicates that its Report should not be construed as restricting the study of religion only to the elementary and undergraduate levels, that "the scholar called to undertake the work should meet a friendly interest in furthering scholarship in his own field."[1]

This Report has been discussed and quoted from at some length because of the inherent value of the Report in its concise and illuminating discussion of the study of religion and in its suggestions regarding approach, points of beginning, and manner and areas of further development, and because of its importance to subsequent developments at Princeton. The Report was presented first to the faculty and later to the Board of Trustees of Princeton. On recommendation of the faculty, the Trustees approved the authorization of the suggested courses and the appointment of a standing committee of the faculty to act in lieu of a department and to select and nominate a scholar to conduct the courses.

In the Fall of 1940, five years after the issuance of the Report, George F. Thomas, who had taken honors in theology at Oxford, where he had been a Rhodes Scholar in 1923, who had received his doctor's degree in philosophy at Harvard in 1929, and who had been Professor of Philosophy at Dartmouth and at the University of North Carolina, was appointed Professor of Religious Thought on the Paine Foundation. Professor Thomas began his teaching by giving two full-year courses, one on the Old and New Testaments and the other on the development of Christian Thought.

A clear indication of Dr. Thomas' orientation is evident in his Inaugural Lecture, "Religion in an Age of Secularism," delivered in October, 1940. Noting that the faculty Report of 1935 stressed beginning with the historical approach, Dr. Thomas points to the importance of going beyond this approach to a second stage, that is, to "the establishment of courses which shall face frankly the theoretical problems of religion, especially those of our own time." Professor Thomas argues for this second stage on the basis of the very nature of religion itself as a source of unity and not merely as a segment of historical development of antiquarian interest. " (O)ne of the major tasks of a professor of religious thought in our secular age," he asserts, "should be to restate and reexamine the claim of religion to provide a basis of organic unity." In this connection, he speaks of "the vital necessity of a rediscovery of the Hebraic and Christian tradition," a necessity which the Faculty Committee had itself recognized. The study of religion, Thomas concludes, should not be "exclusively an intellectual affair, aiming at a modicum of knowledge about one of many branches of learning." The history of religion should be regarded as preliminary to coming to grips critically with the issues and problems of the present.[2]

The Princeton faculty approved the establishment of a Department of Religion in 1946, thus bringing to one stage of culmination a process which had begun with the kind of faculty support and direction represented in the Report of 1935, and which had been continued under the able direction of a man of the orientation and critical acumen of Professor Thomas. The establishment of the Department both recognized the obvious interest in the study of religion on the part of Princeton students who had registered in substantial numbers for the courses taught by Professor Thomas and others and indicated, too, the continuing support from the faculty for the independent study of religion.

Courses listed in the early years of the Department's existence included: Introduction to Judaism and **Christianity, and Christian**

Ethics at the 100 level; The Growth of Old Testament Religion, Jesus and New Testament Religion, Christian Ethics and Modern Society, and Problems of Religious Thought at the 200 level; St. Paul and the Early Church, Medieval Christian Thought, The Reformation and the Age of Reason, Religious Thought since 1800, Religion in East and West, and Great Religious Leaders at the 300 level. In 1946 there were only three men on the teaching staff, Professor Thomas, and with him an assistant professor with a special competence in Christian Ethics and an instructor with a special competence in New Testament. Two plans of study (majors) were offered for departmental students, one involving a depth concentration in religion and the other involving a combination of the study of religion and philosophy or religion and history. It was also possible for a student to concentrate in religion under the Special Program in the Humanities.[3]

As departmental enrollments grew, more instructors were added to the teaching staff, new courses were introduced, including Christian Ideas in Literature, Prophetic and Wisdom Literature of the Hebrews, Religions of the Far East and Religions of the Near East and West, and plans for study involving religion and literature and religion and the Special Program in American Civilization were provided.

A very significant step was taken with the announcement in 1955 of a graduate program leading to the Ph.D. degree in religion. Three additional full professors were added to an already augmented staff, one in Old Testament, one in New Testament and one in Church History, or the History of Christianity. This step had been planned for some time, and to a degree had even been anticipated by the Report of 1935. It was made possible with the aid of grants from the James and the Danforth Foundations.

The 1955 Announcement of the graduate program states that it is the purpose of graduate work in the Department "to further the development of scholarship in religion and to help men prepare themselves to teach religion, and its relation to other fields of study, in colleges and universities." The basic requirement for admission is stated to be "the same preparation in religion as that required for the Bachelor's Degree in the Department of Religion at Princeton." Where deficiencies appear to exist a student is required to enroll as a "Qualifying Graduate Student in undergraduate courses or in courses offered at Princeton Theological Seminary before being admitted to the status of a fully qualified graduate student." Students who meet this basic requirement, whether through adequate work at the undergraduate level or through study in an accredited theological seminary, are admitted as fully qualified graduate students and may take the General Examination after two years of study.

The 1955 Announcement indicates that the General Examination, "normally taken at the end of the second year of graduate study, is designed to test the comprehensive knowledge of the student and also his specialized knowledge in the field in which he plans to write his dissertation." Examinations were required in four of six fields, including fields 1 and 2:

1. The Literature and Theology of the Bible.
2. Church History and History of Christian Thought.
3. Philosophy of Religion.
4. History of Religions.
5. Systematic Theology.
6. Christian Ethics.

A fifth examination was required in some aspect of one other subject and the relation of religion to it, such as art, English, history, music, or philosophy.

Graduate courses listed in the 1955 Announcement include: Studies in Old Testament History and Literature, Studies in Old Testament Religion and Theology, Studies in the Gospels, Studies in the New Testament Epistles, Biblical Theology, Early Church History, Medieval Church History, Problems in Church History, Medieval Christian Thought, The Renaissance and Reformation, The Theology of the Reformers, Modern Church History, Studies in the Philosophy of Religion, Problems of the Philosophy of Religion, Religions of the Middle and Far East, Fundamental Elements in the Religions of Mankind, Contemporary Theological Issues, Interpretations of Christian Ethics, and Problems of Christian Ethics. In addition, certain relevant junior and senior undergraduate courses are mentioned as well as a host of courses in "allied departments."

Certain changes in the graduate program have been instituted since its beginning in 1955.[4] The number of required examinations for the General Examination has been reduced from five to four and the options have been altered, both of these steps being taken so as to allow for greater concentration while not relinquishing the goal of breadth. Two additional fields of concentration have been added, in Hinduism and Buddhism in place of the History of Religions generally. This step was made possible with the addition of another full professor to the staff with a special competence in Buddhism. The present requirement for the General Examination includes four parts, three in religion (including the special field) and a fourth in a discipline external to the Department but related to the special field. The three fields in religion are chosen from the following groups:

A.
Old Testament
New Testament

B.
History of Christianity
Theology and Ethics
Philosophy of Religion

C.
Hinduism
Buddhism
History of Religions

A field of concentration is chosen from one of the following: Old Testament, New Testament, History of Christianity, Systematic Theology, Christian Ethics, Philosophy of Religion, or History of Religions (including intensive study of Hinduism or Buddhism). In Group A of the above listings the non-specialist selects two topics for examination; these may be in either Testament or one in each Testament. In Group B the non-specialists may select any one of the fields for examination. In Group C the non-specialist selects one of three options for examination: (1) one religion in depth (Hinduism or Buddhism); (2) History of Religions and one religion; (3) in exceptional circumstances, two religions.

After passing the General Examination, the candidate prepares a dissertation (not exceeding 300 quarto double-spaced typewritten pages in length, exclusive of bibliography) and must pass a Final Oral Examination on the dissertation.

Since the establishment of the graduate program in 1955, 16 students have elected to specialize in the History of Christianity, 14 in Philosophy of Religion, 5 in Christian Ethics, 4 in each of three fields—New Testament, History of Religions and Systematic Theology, and 3 in Old Testament.

Since its establishment in 1946 the Department of Religion at Princeton has become a well established department which today is moving from the status of a small department to that of a medium-sized department with six full professors, two associate professors, two assistant professors, three instructors, and three assistants on the staff (1963-64), with a total undergraduate enrollment of 610 (Spring, 1964), with 63 departmental students (majors), and with 20 graduate students in residence. Thirty-eight of the departmental students are seniors, 22 are juniors, and 3 are sophomores. The departmental report for 1962-63, issued in June, 1963, indicates that 25 senior departmental students graduated and one failed. Seven of this number concentrated under Plan I, which requires passing three comprehensive examinations chosen from the five areas of Biblical Literature, Christian History and Thought, Religious Ethics and Society, Problems of Religious Thought, and History of Religions, and the writing of a junior paper and a senior thesis. The remaining 19 seniors of 1963 concentrated under Plan II, 2 in Religion and Philosophy, 2 in Religion and History, and 15 in Religion and Literature.

It is interesting to note that most of the departmental students have not expressed a professional interest in religion or a desire to continue to specialize in this area. The fact of the relatively large number of departmental students and the fact that most of them do not choose to specialize beyond the B.A. level should be seen in the context of the strong liberal arts emphasis at Princeton — where, for example, the departments with the most undergraduate majors are English Literature and History. This type of liberal arts emphasis and interest might also explain in part the increasing popularity of the Religion and Literature plan among departmental students in Religion. In fact, much of the success of the Princeton program, at the undergraduate level especially, can be attributed to the strength of the liberal arts or humanistic context at Princeton and to the effective manner in which the study of religion has been related to that context.

Selected Courses

Enrollments in courses in selected years are given in Table XII and educational and bibliographical information on members of the faculty are supplied at the end of this chapter. Some of the courses which have consistently had high enrollments and two or three others of general interest are described in the paragraphs that follow.

Table XII
Enrollments in Undergraduate Courses in Religion:
Princeton University

Course	1956-57		1958-59		1960-61		1961-62		1962-63		1963-64	
(Year and Semester)	I	II	I	II	I	II	I	II	I	II	I	II
Intro. Judaism and Christianity (101)	100		94		90		87		67		82	
Christian Ethics (102)		84		58								
Religion in Contemporary America (102)						101		108		118		134
Old Testament Literature & Religion (201)	76		71		77		80		89		78	
Jesus & Christian Beginnings (202)		114		104		116		155		167		105
Christian Ethics & Modern Society (203)	70		66		95		95			118		
Problems of Religious Thought (204)			93			116		137		161		133
Democracy & Communism (205)*									428			
Religions of Far East (307)	47		25		27							
Man & His Religions (206)								49		66		42
Christianity in Modern Britain† and America (305) (306)			35	28	9		16		17		28	
Prophetic & Wisdom Literature of Hebrews (301) (302)			22	18				24		29		13
Medieval Christian Thought (304) (303)	19		16			15		46	15			
Early Christian Thought (302) (303)	14		22		15		13		23			
Reformation & Age of Reason (304) (306)‡		36		26		20		21		31		33
Religious Thought Since 1800 (305) (307)	36		20		15		10		54		62	
Great Religious Leaders (309) (308)			17		23			7		17		
Religious Ideas in Literature (310) (309)		36		20		70		170		174		104
Principles of Christian Ethics (310)												44

(Continued on Next Page)

TABLE XII (*Continued*)

Course	Year and Semester											
	1956-57		1958-59		1960-61		1961-62		1962-63		1963-64	
	I	II	I	II	I	II	I	II	I	II	I	II
Types of Religious Philosophy (311)					23		38		45			
Judaism (312)						25		34		26		26
Hinayana Buddhism (313)							20		13		31	
Mahayana Buddhism (314)								11		49		79
Hinduism (315)							15				9	
Senior Seminar (506)						13		1		1	1	1
Totals	362	437	334	257	421	406	544	593	910	663	530	610

This listing does not include Oriental Studies 336, The Religion of Islam, which is cross-listed in Religion. The enrollment in the Spring of 1964 was 14. Figures supplied by the Department of Religion.

* Taught by Visiting Professor Reinhold Niebuhr.

† Now Religion in American History.

‡ Now the Reformation and the Counter-Reformation.

Introduction to Judaism and Christianity (Religion 101) has been offered in the Department for many years. As a 100 level course it is open to freshmen. In the Fall semester of 1963-64 this course enrolled 36 freshmen, 37 sophomores, 6 juniors and 3 seniors. Professor M. L. Diamond was the lecturer and course lectures covered the following topics:

A. Origins of the Judeo-Christian Tradition.
   Election and the Mystery of the Covenant: God-Israel-Torah
   Biblical Revelation

B. Judaism
   Authority and Tradition in Judaism
   The Sacred Rhythm of Jewish Life
   Reform Movements in Judaism

C. The Origins of Christianity
   The New Testament and Its Message
   The Development of the Church and the Creeds

D. Roman Catholicism
   The Doctrine of the Church
   Earthly Striving and Eternal Destiny

E. Protestantism
    The Reformation
    The Unity of Protestant Affirmation
    The Breadth of Protestant Concerns

Readings were assigned from a wide variety of sources including: the Bible; Bainton, *Early Christianity;* Brantl, *Catholicism;* Brown, *The Spirit of Protestantism;* Dodd, *The Bible Today;* Wouk, *This is my God;* Adam, *the Spirit of Catholicism;* Cohen, *Everyman's Talmud;* Cohon, *Judaism in Theory and Practice;* Dillenberger and Welch, *Protestant Christianity;* Dostoyevski, *The Brothers Karamazov;* Greene, *The Power and the Glory;* Paton, *Cry, the Beloved Country;* Samuel, *The Prince of the Ghetto;* Sandmel, *The Hebrew Scriptures;* and Tillich, *The Protestant Era.* Two 1,500 word papers were required, one based on either *The Power and the Glory* or *Prince of the Ghetto* and the other based on either *The Brothers Karamazov,* Bk. V, chaps. 4 and 5, or *Cry, the Beloved Country.*

Literature and Religion of the Old Testament (Religion 201), taught by Professor R. B. Y. Scott, enrolled 78 students in the Fall semester, 1963-64—9 freshmen, 37 sophomores, 24 juniors, and 8 seniors. The course outline included the following topics: Introduction to Old Testament Studies; Moses, the Exodus and Israel's Covenant with Yahweh; Sagas of the Patriarchs; the Mythology of Beginnings; History and Religion from Joshua to Elisha; Classical Hebrew Prophecy— (i) Amos and Hosea, (ii) Isaiah and Micah; the Deuteronomic Reform, Jeremiah, the Exile; Second Isaiah and the Suffering Servant; Prophetic Eschatology—the Messianic King; Old Testament Poetry and Psalms; Sages and Sceptics—Proverbs and Ecclesiastes; and the Book of Job. Readings were assigned from the following works: the Revised Standard Version of the Bible; Anderson, *Understanding the Old Testament;* the *Interpreter's Bible;* Bright, *History of Israel;* Buber, *The Prophetic Faith;* Grollenberg, *Atlas of the Bible*; Hooke, *In the Beginning;* Klausner, *The Messianic Idea in Israel;* Lindblom, *Prophecy in Ancient Israel;* May, *Oxford Bible Atlas;* Macleish, "*J. B.*"; McCasland, *Religion of the Bible;* Mowinkel, *He that Cometh;* Muilenburg, *The Way of Israel;* Napier, *From Faith to Faith;* Rowley, *The Growth of the Old Testament;* Sandmel, *The Hebrew Scriptures;* R. B. Y. Scott, *The Psalms as Christian Praise* and *The Relevance of the Prophets;* Terrien, *Job, Poet of Existence* and *The Psalms and Their Meaning;* and Wright, *Biblical Archaeology.*

Jesus and Christian Beginnings (Religion 202), a standard and popular offering for many years, enrolled 167 students in the Spring of 1963, including 31 freshmen, 88 sophomores, 37 juniors and 11 seniors. Professor Franklin Young was the lecturer and the topics discussed included: The World of the Early Church: Graeco-Roman and Jewish Background; the Emergence of the Christian Community; The Synoptic Gospels; the Gospel before the Gospels; the Gospel of Mark; the Mission and Message of Jesus: the Kingdom of God, the Ethic of the Kingdom, His Vocation and Death; the Church of Jerusalem and the Apostle Paul; the Apostle and the Gentile Mission; the Death of Paul: the Decline of Jewish Christianity; the Post-Apostolic Church: Conflict and Development; and a Reinterpretation of the Gospel: The Gospel of John. Readings were assigned from: the Revised Standard Version of the Bible; Bornkamm, *Jesus of Nazareth;* Kee and Young, *Understanding the New Testament; Gospel Parallels* (Nelson) ; Allmen, *A Companion to the Bible;* Bultmann, *Primitive Christianity in its Contemporary Setting;* Dibelius, *Jesus;* Dibelius and Kummel, *Paul;* Dodd, *The Apostolic Preaching and its Development;* Fuller, *The New Testament in Current Study;* Grant, *The Gospels: Their Origin and Growth;* the *Interpreters Bible;* Price, *Interpreting the New Testament;* and Wright and Filson, *The Westminster Historical Atlas.*

Christian Ethics and Modern Society (Religion 203), taught by Professor Paul Ramsey, has also been a consistently popular course. The enrollment in the Fall of 1963-64 was 118, including 7 freshmen, 54 sophomores, 27 juniors and 30 seniors. Topics discussed in the course included Sex and Related Problems, Race Relations, Christian-Political Theories, Communism, and War. Readings were assigned from Baldwin, *The Fire Next Time;* Bennett, *Christianity and Communism Today;* Fletcher, *Morals and Medicine;* King, *Stride Toward Freedom;* Maritain, *Man and the State;* Niebuhr, *The Children of Light and the Children of Darkness;* Ramsey, *War and the Christian Conscience* and *Christian Ethics and the Sit-In; Seven Great* (Papal) *Encyclicals;* and St. John-Stevas, *Life, Death and the Law.*

Problems of Religious Thought (Religion 204) taught by Professor George Thomas, had an enrollment of 161 in the Spring of 1963—57 freshmen, 70 sophomores, 19 juniors and 15 seniors. The outline of topics is as follows:

I. Introduction
    1. Philosophy and Religion
    2. The Nature of Religion

II. Western Religious Thought
  3. Medieval Christian Theism
  4. Modern Skepticism
  5. Religious Humanism and the Scientific Revolution

III. Contemporary Approaches to God
  6. Faith and its Grounds
  7. Religious Experience and Insight
  8. Philosophical Reflection
  9. Revelation
  10. Religious Language: Myth, Symbol and Analogy

IV. The Nature and Destiny of Man
  11. The Nature of Man
  12. The Problem of Evil
  13. Freedom and Grace

Readings were assigned from Temple, *Nature, Man and God;* Abernethy and Langford, *Philosophy of Religion;* Heschel, *God in Search of Man;* Butterfield, *Christianity and History;* Otto, *The Idea of the Holy;* Burtt, *Types of Religious Philosophy;* Copleston, *Aquinas;* Baumer, *Religion and the Rise of Scepticism;* Sullivan, *The Limitations of Science;* Herberg, *Judaism and Modern Man;* Newman, *A Grammar of Assent;* and Thomas, *Christian Ethics and Moral Philosophy.*

Man and His Religions (Religion 206), taught by Professor Philip H. Ashby, had an enrollment of 66 in the Spring of 1963—15 freshmen, 27 sophomores, 16 juniors and 8 seniors. The outline of topics is as follows:

I. The Study of Religion

II. Ancient Religious Themes
  Egyptian and Semitic
  The Far East
  The Middle East
  The Near East and the West

III. Classical Religious Themes
  India
  Hinduism
  Buddhism
  Islam
  The Mystical Motif
  The Soteriological Motif

Readings were assigned from: Andrae, *Mohammed: The Man and His Faith;* Eliade, *The Sacred and the Profane;* Frankfort, *Ancient Egyptian Religion;* Malinowski, *Magic, Science and Religion;* Stace, *The Teachings of the Mystics;* Zimmer, *Philosophies of India;* and Van der Leeuw, *Religion in Essence and Manifestation.*

Religious Thought Since 1880 (Religion 307), taught by Professor Arthur C. McGill, had an enrollment of 62 in the Fall of 1963-64—5 sophomores, 22 juniors and 35 seniors. The outline of topics is as follows:

I. Background: The Problem of Rational Evidence
II. Subjectivity: The Problem of Man
   Schleiermacher, Feuerbach, Nietzsche, Schweitzer and Otto
III. Beyond the Human
   The Answer to Feuerbach, Barth
   Man's Sinfulness, Niebuhr
   Release from Myth and Fact, Bultmann
   The Reaffirmation of Man, Barth

Readings were assigned from Macintosh, *Types of Modern Theology;* Paine, *The Age of Reason;* Schleiermacher, *The Christian Faith;* Feuerbach, *The Essence of Christianity;* Nietzsche, *The Portable Nietzsche;* Schweitzer, *The Quest of the Historical Jesus;* Otto, *The Idea of the Holy;* Barth, *Epistle to the Romans, The Humanity of God,* and *Church Dogmatics;* Niebuhr, *The Nature and Destiny of Man;* Bultmann, *Jesus Christ and Mythology;* and Baumer, *Religion and the Rise of Scepticism.*

Religious Ideas in Literature (Religion 309), taught by visiting Professor W. R. Mueller, had an enrollment of 104 in the Fall of 1963-64—27 sophomores, 53 juniors and 24 seniors. Readings and discussion topics were based on the following: Camus, *The Plague;* Sartre, *Nausea* and *No Exit;* Ionesco, *Four Plays;* Orwell, *1984;* Milton, *Paradise Lost;* Eliot, *The Complete Poems and Plays;* Faulkner, *Light in August;* Kafke, *The Trial;* Silone, *Bread and Wine;* Beckett, *Waiting for Godot* or *Endgame;* Greene *The Power and the Glory* or *The Heart of the Matter;* Hemingway, *A Farewell to Arms* or *The Sun Also Rises* or *The Old Man and the Sea;* Williams, *The Glass Menagerie* or *A Streetcar Named Desire.*

Judaism (Religion 312), a course offered regularly since the Spring of 1960, had an enrollment of 26 in the Spring of 1963—5 sophomores, 12 juniors and 9 seniors. Professor Malcolm Diamond was the lecturer and the topics discussed included: The Bible; Survival; the Terminology of the Talmud, Halachah: Torah as regulating Life; Haggadah: the teachings of the Rabbis; Judaism in the Diaspora; Lurianic Mysticism: Exile and Reunion; Hasidism; Religion of Crisis; Revelation and History; Paradox without Anguish; Judaism in America. Readings were assigned from the Bible; Adler, *The World of the Talmud;* Mamberger, *The Bible: A Modern Jewish Approach;* Buber, *The Way of Man;* Glatzer, *The Hammer on the Rock;* Glazer, *American Judaism;* Goldin, *The Living Talmud;* Herberg, *Judaism and Modern Man;* Kegley and Bretall, *Reinhold Niebuhr;* Roth, *History of the Jews;* Scholem, *Major Trends in Jewish Mysticism;* Schwarz, ed., *Great Ages and Ideas of the Jewish People;* and Buber, *Moses* or *The Prophetic Faith.*

Other courses open to undergraduates, but not described here, include: Religion in Contemporary America (102), Studies in Theology (302), Early Christianity (303), Medieval Christian Thought (304), Christianity in Modern Britain and America (305), The Reformation and the Age of Reason (306), Great Religious Leaders (308), Principles of Christian Ethics (310), Types of Religious Philosophy (311), Hinayana Buddhism (313), Mahayana Buddhism (314), Hinduism (315), and The Religion of Islam (Oriental Studies, 336). It is of interest to note that the courses on Hinayana Buddhism, Mahayana Buddhism, and Hinduism, only recently introduced, immediately attracted more than enough student interest to be offered. In fact, the enrollment in Mahayana Buddhism was 79 in the Spring of 1964 and the enrollment in Hinayana Buddhism was 31 in the Fall of 1963-64.

A notable feature of the Princeton system of undergraduate instruction is the preceptorial conference, a method used generally in upperclass courses in the humanities and social sciences, and in many underclass courses. The weekly preceptorial conference, involving usually less than 10 students and a faculty member or teaching assistant, supplements the course lectures. The conference involves discussion of some prearranged topic or selected reading. The preceptorial is described as "an exploratory undertaking for both student and instructor." Nearly all of the religion courses at the 200 and 300 levels involve two lectures per week plus a preceptorial conference. Religion 101 and 102 also meet for two lectures each week and classes are sectioned into groups of 12 to 15 students which meet with a class instructor once each week. Princeton also designates a two-week period near the end of each semester as a Reading Period when no classes are held but students and faculty are expected to be on campus.

The graduate courses in Religion listed in the most recent announcement are much the same as those listed in the Announcement of 1955 (listed above) excepting that Religions of the Middle and Far East is not listed whereas separate courses in Hinduism and Buddhism have been added (as noted above) and a course in Biblical Texts has also been added. Graduate courses ordinarily meet once a week in a three-hour session.

Conclusions

The breadth and depth of the offerings in religion at Princeton are impressive—perhaps especially so to the observer who is more familiar with the limited and scattered offerings in religion which is more the rule than the exception in so many American universities. A combination of factors accounts for the Princeton "success story." These include careful planning from the beginning, the exercise of considerable care in the selection of faculty, the twofold orientation— toward historical factors and contemporary issues, friendly interest on the part of many of the University faculty and support from the administration, interest among students which has been captured and developed further by an imaginative curricular program and a stimulating faculty in Religion, the development of a graduate program which has had the effect of making undergraduate offerings richer and more extensive, the stress on the humanities and the liberal arts which remains strong at Princeton, and the presence of the necessary financial support to develop a comprehensive program of quality.

The Princeton program might become even more comprehensive and exciting with the addition of scholars in Roman Catholic and Jewish studies, scholars primarily interested in these movements and systems of thought *as religions.* As a matter of fact, there is considerable hope that such appointments may be made in the near future.

Religion has been firmly recognized as part of the humanities area at Princeton and this orientation is abundantly evident in course offerings and in plans for departmental students, including the recently instituted Religion and Art or Architecture combination. Religion is, indeed, a humanistic field, but one might also look for some greater degree of liaison with the social sciences or some more interest of a social science nature than presently appears to exist. It is interesting to note, for example, the absence of work in Sociology of Religion, although some of the courses in Religion obviously draw on materials and concepts from this sub-discipline.

Some observers might want to argue that the area divisions in the graduate program bear an undue resemblance to the divisions of

Protestant seminary-based graduate programs in religion. The basic question is not, however, one of resemblance or lack thereof to any other type of graduate program but what is required by the subject and the disciplines engaged in the study of it. On this point Professor Ramsey, former chairman of the Princeton Department and a member of the faculty since 1944, argues that area divisions in the Princeton graduate program "have their own integrity wherever they may be taught or studied." He rightly asserts that the "division of subject matter and the appropriate methods of research arise from the nature of religion as a scholarly discipline."[5] The points at issue in the structuring of any graduate program in Religion are what subject matter to stress in this vast and complex field, which methodologies of the various relevant methodologies (historical, literary-critical, archaeological, anthropological, sociological, philosophical, and theological) to emphasize, and how to balance grounding in methods with content mastery. By stressing both breadth and depth the Princeton program seeks to expose the student to methodology and content in various relevant areas and to ground him more thoroughly in one specific area. As Professor Ramsey suggests, the most obvious test of the relative success of this program will be the teaching and future scholarly careers of the students who have gone through it.

Biographical and Bibliographical Information, Department of Religion Faculty; Princeton University—1963-64

PHILIP HARRISON ASHBY, *Associate Professor*

B. 1916. College of Puget Sound, B.A. 1938; Pacific School of Religion, B.D. 1943; Chicago, Ph.D. 1950.

Teacher: Princeton, 1950-.

Author: The Conflict of Religions, 1955; *History and Future of Religious Thought,* 1963.

KENNETH K. S. CH'EN, *Professor*

B. 1907. Hawaii, B.A. 1931; Yenching, M.A. 1934; Harvard, Ph.D., 1946.

Teacher: Yenching, 1935-36; Hawaii, 1936-40; Yenching, 1947-50; Harvard, 1950-58; UCLA 1958-61; Princeton, 1961-.

Author: The Svagata Story in the Divyavadana, 1947; *Anti-Buddhist Propaganda During the Nan Chao,* 1952; *Apropos the Mendhaka Story,* 1953; *Economic Background of the Hui-Chang Suppression of Buddhism in China,* 1956; *Buddhism in China: A Historical Survey,* 1964.

HORTON DAVIES, *Professor*

B. 1916. Edinburgh, M.A. (Honors) 1937, B.D. (Honors) 1940; Oxford, Ph.D. 1943.

Teacher: Rhodes University, Grahamstown, South Africa, 1946-53; Mansfield College, Oxford, 1953-56; Princeton, 1956-, Guggenheim Fellow, 1959-60.

Author: Christian Worship: Its Making and Meaning, 1946; *The Worship of the English Puritans,* 1948; *The English Free Churches,* 1952, 1963; *Christian Deviations,* 1954; *A Mirror of the Ministry in Modern Novels,* 1959; *Worship and Theology in England,* vol. III, 1961; vol. IV, 1962; *Challenge of the Sects,* 1962; *Varieties of English Preaching,* 1963.

MALCOLM LURIA DIAMOND, *Associate Professor*

B. 1924. Yale, B.E. 1945; Trinity College, Cambridge, 1947-48; Columbia, Ph.D. 1956.

Teacher: Sarah Lawrence, 1950-51; Washington Square College, New York University, 1951-53; Princeton, 1953-.

Author: Martin Buber, Jewish Existentialist, 1960.

WILLIAM PAUL JONES, *Assistant Professor*

B. 1930. Mt. Union College, A.B. 1951; Yale, B.D. 1954, M.A. 1955, Ph.D. 1960.

Teacher: Princeton, 1958-.

Author: The Recovery of Life's Meaning, Understanding Creation and the Incarnation, 1963; 8 articles in *Masterpieces of World Philosophy,* 1960-61; 4 articles in *Masterpieces of Christian Thought,* 1963.

ARTHUR CHUTE McGILL, *Assistant Professor*

B. 1926. Harvard, B.A. 1947; Yale, B.D. 1951, Ph.D. 1960.

Teacher: Wesleyan University, 1955-59; Princeton, 1960-.

Author: The Place of Dogmatic Theology in the University, 1960; *Celebration of the Flesh: Poetry in Christian Life,* 1964.

ROBERT PAUL RAMSEY, *Professor*

B. 1913. Millsaps, B.S. 1935; Yale, B.D. 1940, Ph.D. 1943.

Teacher: Millsaps, 1937-39; Garrett Biblical Institute, 1942-44; Princeton, 1944-.

Author: Basic Christian Ethics, 1950; *Jonathan Edwards, Freedom of the Will,* ed., 1957; *War and the Christian Conscience,* 1961; *Christian Ethics and the Sit-in,* 1961; *Nine Modern Moralists,* 1962.

ROBERT BALGARNIE YOUNG SCOTT, *Professor*

B. 1899. Toronto, B.A. 1922, M.A. 1924, Ph.D. 1928; Knox College, Toronto, B.D. 1926.

Teacher: Union College of British Columbia, 1928-31; United Theological College, Montreal, 1931-48; McGill University, 1948-55; Princeton, 1955-.

Author: Relevance of the Prophets, 1944; *Treasures from Judean Caves,* 1955; *The Psalms as Christian Praise,* 1958; *Isaiah* 1-39, *Interpreter's Bible;* Articles in symposia and Bible Dictionaries.

GEORGE FINGER THOMAS, *Professor*

B. 1899. Southern Methodist University, B.A. 1919; Rhodes Scholar, Oxford, B.A. 1923; Harvard, Ph.D. 1929; Kenyon College, S.T.D. (Honorary) 1951; Southern Methodist University, L.L.D. (Honorary).

Teacher: Southern Methodist University, 1923-25; Swarthmore, 1927-31; Dartmouth, 1931-37; University of North Carolina, 1937-40; Princeton, 1940-.

Author: Spirit and Its Freedom, 1938; *Poetry, Religion and the Spiritual Life,* 1951; *Christian Ethics and Moral Philosophy,* 1955; *The Vitality of the Christian Tradition,* ed., 1944.

FRANKLIN WOODROW YOUNG, *Professor*

B. 1915. Dartmouth, B.A. 1937; Crozer, B.D. 1942; Duke, Ph.D. 1946.

Teacher: Duke, 1944-50; Yale, 1950-54; Episcopal Theological Seminary of the Southwest, 1954-59; Princeton, 1959-.

Author: With Howard Kee, *Understanding the New Testament,* 1957. Articles, *Interpreter's Bible Dictionary; Encyclopedia Britannica,* contributor.

---

1. *Princeton University Report of the Special Committee of the Faculty on Religious Education,* April 11, 1935. The members of the committee were P. A. Chapman, T. M. Greene, C. S. Osgood, R. M. Scoon, T. J. Wertenbaker, and A. M. Friend, Jr., Chairman.

2. This lecture was printed and distributed by Princeton University.

3. Course titles and requirements for majors taken from announcements and catalogues, Princeton University, 1946-.

4. A detailed description of the graduate program can be found in Professor Paul Ramsey's article on "Princeton University's Graduate Program in Religion," *The Journal of Bible and Religion,* vol. XXX, No. 4, October, 1962, pp. 291-298.

5. *Ibid.,* p. 294.

CONCLUSION

THE ADVANCEMENT OF THE STUDY OF RELIGION IN AMERICAN UNIVERSITIES

Obviously religion is being studied in American universities, including state universities. And a variety of structural patterns have been developed for this study, some of which are more adequate to the subject and more in keeping with the nature of the university than others. But at the completion of this case study of ten institutions two broader conclusions can be reached: (1) the study of religion has not achieved the degree of precision in methodology and thoroughness of scholarship which the subject warrants; and (2) the study of this subject is still in an underdeveloped state in American universities, and especially in state universities. These are actually two sides of the same coin. On the one hand, more adequate scholarship in religion will presumably bring greater university interest in developing the field. On the other hand, such interest is needed if more specialized scholarship is to be achieved.

Professor Paul Ramsey has likened the status of religion as an academic field today to that of "natural philosophy" a century ago when a wide variety of subjects, now studied in such disciplines as botany, chemistry, physics, and zoology, were all studied under this one heading.[1] Religion is just such a complex and diffuse subject. The further development of this field is dependent upon more intensive work in its various divisions, more careful attention to the methodologies appropriate to the study of religious phenomena, and more specialized studies of these phenomena. One has the impression that some graduate programs in religion tend to stress the mastery of vast amounts of subject matter while slighting the mastery of tools and methods for the systematic and detailed study of such subject matter. No doubt a broad survey of the field is helpful because of the complexity and pervasiveness of religion as a human phenomenon, but a rigorous grounding in the methods of critical analysis and investigation is even more necessary if significant scholarly work is to result. An overly generalized approach in a graduate program may, however, be in part the result of the practical situation confronting the young scholar in religion. Frequently he may be expected to "cover" a broad field in his teaching and seldom afforded an opportunity to develop his own area of specialization.

While the study of religion has been on the increase in American universities in the past two decades, the current situation is one in which this area continues to be an underdeveloped one. This is evident in a comparison of the opportunities for study and research in religion with similar opportunities for study and research in other fields of culture such as art or politics. An examination of the status in American universities of the disciplines and sub-disciplines directly engaged in the study of religion will add further support to the statement. Sociology of religion, psychology of religion, and anthropology of religion occupy minor and insignificant roles in their "parent" disciplines. The history of religions is a discipline which receives adequate attention and support in no more than three or four major American universities. While the vast majority of American universities offer some kind of work in Biblical studies, the number with recognized Biblical scholars on their faculties is very small and opportunities for advanced study in this area are confined largely to a few universities with theological faculties. And theological studies are largely untouched in most state universities.

What is needed at this juncture is systematic encouragement of scholarly work in religion, fuller development of the disciplines directly concerned with the study of this area, and imaginative efforts to realize the potential in it. This is a task for the universities. The subject is broad and complex enough, and the methodologies involved are varied enough, to demand and warrant a variety of approaches. Institutions obviously vary in their capacity to support concentrated study of one particular religious tradition or another, or to encourage the intensive development of one or more of the disciplines and sub-disciplines engaged in the study of religion. Furthermore, some institutions can more easily engage in bold experimentation in this area than can others.

But while variety is quite natural and desirable, one would hope that universities would take seriously their responsibilities for the study of religion and that the same basic operational principles would be applied in this area as in other academic areas. Scholarship, rooted in technical competence and involving critical analysis and synthesis, is the touchstone of the academic community. That such scholarship should inform the study of religion, as it does the study of other areas, is elemental. However, that this is the case in American universities is not entirely evident. All too frequently the study of religion is approached in an off-handed manner, becoming the task of those whose primary scholarly competence and interest lie in other areas. Examine, for example, the manner in which the Bible is studied and taught—even as literature—in many American universities. While it is expected as a matter of course that the teacher of French literature should obviously know the cultural context and language of his materials, the teacher of Biblical literature often does not know Greek and Hebrew and may have little familiarity with Biblical scholarship. Or consider the fairly common practice of relegating the courses in religion to the philosophy department. While it is evident that the philosophy of religion is a legitimate area of scholarship, it is also evident that such a scholar almost of necessity must have some competence in theology if he is to do justice to his field. It is not evident, however, that training in philosophy, especially when such training is heavily weighted in the direction of logic and language analysis, qualifies a person to teach history of religions or comparative religion. But, quite naturally, the philosophy department is likely to be interested in employing someone who is first of all trained in philosophy, and whatever he may do in the study of or teaching about religion will probably be of secondary concern to him and will not reflect the scholarly depth which any field as significant as religion demands.

Given the complex nature of the modern university, it is quite obvious that the proper scholarly development of any area or field requires some sort of core or center. Such a core does not guarantee quality work, but the chance of producing quality work appears to be better with than without it. The standard core in the academic community is the department, organized to develop a discipline or area. Other types of academic organization which may operate with some effectiveness include the "institute," the "center," and the "special program." The success of any of these patterns depends on such factors as cohesiveness of interest and direction, budgetary support, and effectiveness of administrative action, as well as quality of work. The interdepartmental faculty committee in religious studies may also operate effectively, but this type of arrangement is usually more successful in dealing with short range programs or projects than with those requiring persistent attention over several years.

The core or center is necessary not only for administrative reasons but also to encourage the proper *scholarly* development of a discipline or field. Central to the idea or model of a university is the notion of groups of scholars exercising and developing their own disciplines. This rests on the assumption that it is the scholars in a particular area who are best qualified to determine what is significant in that area; what should be conserved and passed on to students; what is irrelevant; and what is worthy of further investigation.

The university which does not have some core concerned primarily with the study of religion is not really taking this subject very seriously. Whether this core be the standard type of department or some other mechanism is not as important as the fact that it exist. And in religion, as in other areas, the scholars in the field should be the ones with the major voice in determining how the field is developed.

As a complex field religion offers a challenge to the ingenuity of the university. Since it is a major factor in human life and culture, provision for its study is a significant test of a university's inclusiveness. In fact, what a university does with the study of religion, and especially of the more sensitive aspects of this subject, is one important measure of its autonomy and freedom.[2]

---

1. "Theological Studies in College and Seminary," *Theology Today*, XVII (January 1961), p. 472.

2. See James Alfred Martin, Jr., "A Universal Mission of the University: Appropriate Study of Religious and Political Traditions," *Christianity and Crisis*, XXIV (March 16, 1964), pp. 37-40.

APPENDIX I
RELIGION IN A STATE UNIVERSITY SYSTEM

The following is a memorandum from the Office of the President of the University of California to the members of the Committee on Educational Policy of the Academic Senate and dealing with the "Role of the University in Teaching and Research with Reference to Religion." The memorandum is dated April 12, 1963. It is reproduced here with the permission of the Office of the President of the University of California:

During the past year the discussion and study concerning the role of religion at the University of California has emphasized two areas: (1) the aspects of religion related to campus life, and (2) the role of the University in teaching and research in religion. At the request of the President, the Academic Council prepared a report on these areas, dated February 21, 1962, which was submitted to the Regents' Committee on Educational Policy at its June 1962 meeting. At that meeting, the President reported that he was establishing, after advice of the Academic Senate and the Chief Campus Officers, the guidelines of University policy concerning the role of religion in campus life.

In regard to the role of the University in teaching and research in religion, the President also reported at the June 1962 meeting that he had requested the Chief Campus Officers on the Berkeley, Davis, Los Angeles, Riverside, and Santa Barbara campuses, in consultation with appropriate Academic Senate committees, to: (a) review the academic offerings in the area of religion with special attention to the adequacy of work in comparative religion, (b) recommend as to whether additional courses should be offered, and (c) recommend concerning the establishment of a department of Comparative Religion.

The purpose of this report is to summarize the campus reports received in reply to the above.

Berkeley Campus

The Berkeley Committee on Courses lists 60 courses in the area of religion, six of which are concerned entirely with aspects of religion. At present, Berkeley does not offer a course in comparative religion. It does, however, offer a program whereby a student can study religion in a department of the College of Letters and Science germane to the purpose or propose an individual major. This program has been available for a number of years but has had few students. As a result of the study on teaching and research in religion, the Committee on

Courses recommends (1) that the Berkeley campus offer a course in Comparative Religion, (2) that the faculty study the possibility of a group major in religion, and (3) that the establishment of a department of religion be opposed. Chancellor Strong concurs with the above recommendations.

Davis Campus

The Davis report described five courses in the area of religion and the academic offerings of the Department of History, English, and Dramatic Art in which the majority of courses contain varying degrees of religious thought and expression. In three courses, including a course in Comparative Religion, the religious content is the total or predominant part of the course program. The Davis report did not discuss proposed courses or programs except to mention that a sociology of religion course will be offered when a qualified staff member can be appointed. The possible creation of a Department of Religion was referred to the Davis Committee on Educational Policy. Chancellor Mark states, "There is a consensus of opinion on our campus that such courses should be continued within existing departments."

Los Angeles Campus

The Los Angeles Committee on Courses lists 30 courses dealing directly or indirectly with religion. Three courses, including a course in Comparative Religion, are concerned entirely with religious thought and expression. The Committee on Courses feels that academic offerings in religion are adequate and does not recommend any effort to increase the number of courses in religion; however, Chancellor Murphy notes that a scholar in early Christian Church history will join the faculty next fall and that a distinguished Islamic scholar may be appointed to the faculty. The Committee on Courses recommends very strongly that no Department of Comparative Religion be created on the Los Angeles campus.

Riverside Campus

The Riverside Educational Policy Committee lists four courses in the regular academic curriculum and the Departments of History, Art, Music, Literature, and Philosophy in which the majority of courses contain varying degrees of religious thought and expression. Two courses are entirely concerned with aspects of religion. In 1954 a course entitled Comparative Religion was offered in University Extension; it is considered ancestral to the present course in Primitive

Religion. The Educational Policy Committee considers current academic offerings adequate and is not prepared to initiate a Department of Comparative Religion at this time. The Riverside Academic Advisory Council concurs with the findings and recommendations of the Educational Policy Committee.

Santa Barbara Campus

The Santa Barbara campus offers thirteen courses in the area of religion, ten of which are concerned entirely with religious thought and expression. In June, the Divisional Academic Senate approved the establishment of a Religious Institutions major. The major is designed for students desiring a general education with emphasis upon this aspect of western civilization and comparative cultures. The Santa Barbara Committee on Educational Policy feels that work offered in Comparative Religion is more than adequate, although the creation of a staff more centrally devoted to this field is desirable. Professor Paul Tillich, who is participating in the program this year, represents the type of scholarship envisaged for the program at Santa Barbara by the Committee on Religious Institutions. The Committee on Educational Policy does not believe it opportune to consider now the creation of a separate department, such as a Department of Comparative Religion.

APPENDIX II
THE GRADUATE THEOLOGICAL UNION
Berkeley and San Anselmo, California

The Graduate Theological Union was established in 1962. According to its Articles of Incorporation, it was

> formed to conduct an educational institution offering instruction on the graduate theological level; to participate with theological seminaries and other institutions of higher learning in cooperative programs of study, and to grant such academic degrees and honors as are customarily granted in universities and seminaries of learning, either in its own name only, or in conjunction with another such institution.

Five Protestant theological seminaries in Berkeley and San Anselmo initially founded the Graduate Theological Union and its faculty was drawn from these institutions. The By-Laws of the G.T.U. provide that "Any academic institution providing professional training for the Bachelor's Degree in Divinity or substantially equivalent instruction in the field of Theology may . . . apply for acceptance as a participating institution. . . ." Degree programs leading to the Th.D. and Ph.D. degrees are offered by the G.T.U.

The G.T.U. is of special interest in this context because of its relationships with the Graduate Division of the University of California at Berkeley. These relationships are largely informal; neither the University nor the Graduate Division at Berkeley has entered into any formal agreement with the G.T.U. However, after discussions with proper committees and administrators, the Dean of the Graduate Division at Berkeley has indicated that qualified graduate students in the G.T.U. may be accepted for course work at Berkeley and that faculty members at Berkeley may participate in the direction of degree students in the G.T.U. if they choose to do so. Two Berkeley faculty members, Professor Charles Y. Glock of Sociology and Associate Professor Paul Seabury of Political Science, have been appointed by the Dean of the Graduate Division to serve in a liaison capacity between the G.T.U. and the Graduate Division of the University of California, Berkeley. Application from G.T.U. students to take course work on the Berkeley campus of the University will be referred to these men and, if approved by them, to the Dean for final approval. In effect, such students will be granted the status of special graduate students. As such, they will not need to be approved by any academic department at Berkeley and they will not be regarded as degree candidates in that institution. They will, however, be required to pay the normal tuition fees at Berkeley. In the words of the Dean of the Graduate Division, this affords the student the opportunity of having "the best of both worlds."

On the basis of this largely informal arrangement the G.T.U. Announcement (December 20, 1963) indicates that doctoral programs are currently offered with a faculty appointed by the participating seminaries, "and with the cooperation of the faculty of the Graduate Division of the University of California at Berkeley." The Announcement indicates further that the Ph.D. program

> centers in a theological discipline in the context of the university disciplines. Accordingly, approximately half of the work for the Ph.D. program will be taken in a university setting, normally in the Graduate Division of the University of California in Berkeley. This refers to committee direction and examinations as well as to course work.

Opportunities for specialization are indicated in most of the areas of theological work, including Biblical (Old and New Testament), Historical, Philosophy of Religion, Systematics, Religion and Society, etc. "Programs cutting across these areas," according to the Announcement, "may be approved, provided they meet the criteria of coherence and of encouraging adequate competence." Requirements for the degree programs are spelled out in terms of the more or less standard procedures in this regard, including the qualifying examination, language and residence requirements, the comprehensive examination, and the dissertation. Students will normally be asked to take up residence in one of the participating seminaries. The Ph.D. degree will be conferred by the G.T.U. "with the recommendation of" the seminary of residence; the University will not be formally involved in the conferring of the degree.

This development is unique in its relationship with a state university. While the relationship is quite informal, one can see considerable promise in it. The most immediate benefit would appear to be to the graduate theological student who can, under this arrangement, gain access to faculty, library and other resources of a major university. Beyond this, the arrangement could also enhance the graduate work of the participating seminaries and possibly contribute to the scholarly work carried on by the faculty of those institutions. Finally, it could stimulate an increasing scholarly interest in the areas of religion and theology at the University itself.